Tia,

You are my best friend. I can tell you anything. I love you for who you are for you loving me!

Love Van Page ♡

Page, Vivian
1st Edition.
ISBN: 978-1979251624

I Forgive You

Vivian Page

This book is dedicated to Charity and Issa.

"We are Good Kids!" I love you both.

To Ms. Byrd, for your sincere love and affection.

To Natasha Lake, for speaking life into me and pushing me

to my finish line.

To DeMaurio Page.

You are my definition of Love.

CONTENTS

Prologue

I cheesed in the mirror at my brushed teeth.

"All clean!" I said proudly to my sister who stood next to me, desperate to share space at our tiny bathroom vanity. She rolled her neck and retorted, "Fi-nal-ly, your breath was on fire!" My jaw dropped. I put my hand over my mouth to stifle my laugh.

"No, it was not!" I whispered loudly.

"Yes, it was! Yes, it was!" my sister Charity replied, in a sing-song voice as she shook her hips to an imaginary beat. I howled. Charity always made me laugh uncontrollably. She was a natural comedian; so, everything that she said was hilarious to me. I scrunched up my face and danced with her to her new hit song, "Breath on Fire."

Charity sang and stuck her tongue out as we danced playfully around the bathroom. Then she stopped instantly as footsteps neared the bathroom door. The door opened and before I could escape, a smack across my face knocked me backwards and I stumbled to catch myself before toppling over into the bathtub.

"Shut up and finish getting ready!" Shirl grumbled. "And you betta not miss that bus!" My eyes filled with water as I looked up at her. She raised her hand threatening to strike me again and I flinched. "Fix your damn face girl!" She growled, as her eyes burned into me. I looked down at the tiled floor as I wiped the tears off my cheeks and saw the blood dripping from my nose. I stood motionless, terrified of her next move. Her breathing was rugged as she looked around the bathroom. After delivering one more menacing glance, she retreated down the hallway dragging her feet. I whimpered as I held my nose. Tears began to fall down my face. Charity quickly wiped my face with a cloth and handed me a piece of tissue in her hand. "Don't cry Vivi", she whispered, as she rubbed my back slowly. "I'm gonna tell Dad about this, I promise." She said strongly.

I stared out the school bus window as we drove away from Roseland, the ensemble of ghetto, brick buildings we called home. The bricks, fading from neglect and the once pure white frames that surrounded each window, were now dingy and cracked. Clothing lines hung outside each unit and the grass that covered the playground area was brown and scarce. I looked up at the clouds as the bus creaked to another stop and I thought about flying. I always wished that I could fly away from Roseland and never return. I would fly wherever I was happiest and the first place I would stop would be at school.

School was my refuge; I felt safe and secure while I was there. I knew every morning, once I walked into Ms. Byrd's 3rd grade class; it was going to be a great day! I was always welcomed by her smile each morning as she stood alongside her door. She was so beautiful, with her perfectly coiled curls and glowing brown skin. "Good Morning Vivian", she said in a light and airy tone. "Good Morning Ms. Byrd," I replied. It almost seemed like she had special powers to see right through me. No matter how big I smiled, or how I avoided making eye contact, she always knew when something was bothering me. That morning she gave me a head nod as I entered the classroom, which signaled to put my things away and return to her side. Once everyone had settled on the rainbow rug in the middle of the floor, Ms. Byrd smiled at her assistant, and then led me down the hallway.

"How are you feeling today?" She asked softly.

I didn't answer. She slowed her steps.

"Do you want to tell me what's bothering you?" She continued. I shook my head from side to side. She immediately stopped walking, turned to face me and kneeled as she held both of my hands.

"What happened this morning Vivian?" Her brown eyes poured into mine, pleading for me to speak.

"She hit me", I whimpered, fighting back tears as my eyes swelled.

"And where did she hit you?" Ms. Byrd pressed loudly. I touched my nose and then opened my hand to reveal the bloody kleenex I was using. I covered my eyes to hide the tears that began to pour. Ms. Byrd grabbed my hand as she stood up and forcefully pumped down the hallway towards the nurse's office. The door was wide open as we neared it and the nurse showed no sign of surprise when we entered. "Let me go get my notes", the nurse murmured after noticing my tear soaked shirt. She returned quickly, closing the door behind her. She crossed her legs as she plopped down into her chair, then looked at me annoyed.

"Tell her what you told me," Ms. Byrd erupted. "Tell her exactly what happened. I'll be right back."

She snapped. She slammed the door behind her, leaving me all alone with the nurse. "So, what happened to you?" The nurse snarled. She always sounded as if she was holding her nose while she talked. I shrugged and crossed my arms, desperate to disappear. She stood hastily and approached my side, tilting her clipboard in my direction. "On February 3rd, I examined your arms and they were severely bruised. I saw you two days later, which was February 5th because your lip was busted." She popped her gum as she got closer to me. "On February 12th, you had purple marks across your back and legs, you could barely walk when you came in...shall I continue?" I sniffled and shook my head from side to side, feeling embarrassed.

"So, what happened today?" The nurse urged. The silence was eerie as she waited for me to reply. I stared down at my shoes to avoid her gaze. The nurse's door instantly swung open and the principal dragged my sister into the room followed by Ms. Byrd and another woman who seemed unsettled and concerned. The committee of eyes examining me felt intimidating and intrusive. I avoided Charity's glance because I knew I already said too much. I didn't want to get both of us in trouble. Dad said if anyone ever asked us questions, to just lie and say everything was fine. If we didn't, we would get a pop from him and a more severe beating from Shirl when we got home. "Vivian, this is Brenda, she's a social worker here at Montclair," Ms. Byrd assured me. "She wants to ask you a few questions." I panicked. "No! I don't want to answer questions.

Everything is fine...nothing happened... I promise. Can I just go back to class now?" I begged.

"Just a few questions." Brenda, the social worker said softly. I glanced at Charity for guidance. Her stare served as a warning. I immediately broke down, pleading hysterically to go back to class. "Please, please, please, just let me go back to class!" I squealed. Ms. Byrd reached for me. Tears were rolling down my face. She wiped them gently. I looked away from her. "I made it up Ms. Byrd." I stuttered. "I made up the whole thing." She loosened her grip on my arms. My hands were shaking. My teeth chattered in fear. "Vivian, I know you are afraid and you shouldn't have to be," said the social worker. She rubbed my back as my breathing steadied. I finally had the courage to look into Ms. Byrd's eyes again. She embraced me quickly. My heart was hurting and my body was still trembling. Her warmth eased the chills running through me and I melted into her. I always wished that she could have been my mom. As she held me, I thought about the possibility of finally getting away and having a happy family. She pulled back, looked at me, then said softly, "No one should ever make you feel afraid Vivian. Don't you let anyone make you feel bad for telling the truth."

Life doesn't give you the people that you want. It gives you people that you need; to help you, to hurt you, to leave you, and to make you into the person that you were meant to be." - Brenda Jackson

1: *"You don't have to be sad."*

I don't remember the exact day when we met Shirl or when Dad married her but I do remember how I felt the first time that she hugged me. She was standing in the living room, beside our green, velvet couch and she looked completely unsure of why she was there. My sister, Charity and my brother, Brian, had just gotten home from school and we were greeted by Dad's big grin showing all his pearly whites. We just knew he had a great surprise for us! He led us into the living room where Shirl was standing, bent down and said, "Hey, I found you guys a mom!" It was a strange thing for him to say because I thought we already had a mom but we just never saw her. Grandma talked about her a lot and told me that I look more like Dad than her. But Dad always said, "You have your mother's smile", whenever he was holding me close to him.

Shirl stood there, looking down at us and then looked back at Dad for reassurance. Her hair was jet black and slicked back into a tight ponytail. Her cheekbones were strong and she had a slight smirk permanently etched on her face. I couldn't tell if she was trying to smile at me or keep from crying. She had a very slender build but her shoulders slumped a bit and she stood stiffly, like a newly created robot. I stood beside Charity and Brian, then immediately stepped out and extended my hand. "Hi, I'm Vivian!" I squeaked, awaiting her handshake. She didn't move. I curtsied and bowed in front of her, doing my best impression of an actress finishing her play. Charity giggled and I turned around giggling with her. "I'm Shirl." She announced in a shaky, robotic tone. "Could she really be a robot!" I thought. Dad quickly interrupted her, "Make sure that you guys are calling her mom ok? M-o-m!" He enunciated. "Now, go ahead and give her a hug." He hinted by the nod of his head towards her. I reached both my arms out to embrace her. Shirl slowly bent down and leaned her shoulder in towards me. I squeezed my arms around her quickly and I felt how warm and soft she was. I smiled back at Charity as she watched me closely. Shirl placed one of her arms along my side, patted me twice like you would a dog and then backed away. It was almost as if she was grossed out by me touching her. I was sure I must have smelled from playing outside earlier. I stepped back slowly, waiting for her to say something but she didn't. I turned and looked at Charity and Brian and lifted my eyebrows twice. It was my silly way of making them smile. Dad whispered something to Shirl in her ear, then turned back towards us and said loudly:

"Say thank you guys, I found you a mom!"

"Thank you Dad", we replied in unison.

"You're welcome", he said, feeling very proud of himself.

Dad desperately wanted us to be a family, so we did our best to blend in and welcome our new "mom" and her son, Thomas with open arms. It was exciting to have a new brother and someone new to play with. Thomas was my age so we were in the same class together. He was very quiet at school but the complete opposite as soon as we got home. He would jump up out of his seat as soon as we were nearing our bus stop and I could see the excitement in his eyes. I shared the excitement too. When Shirl and Thomas first moved in with us, Shirl would greet us at the bus stop, sometimes with popsicles in her hands. She let us play outside for a little while before coming in to do our homework and eat dinner. She was sweet to us and all the kids in the neighborhood. Our friends always said, we had the best mom. Shirl would chat with the other moms in the morning as they waited for our bus to arrive. She always made sure her hair was nice and makeup was on before she walked outside with us. We almost missed the bus one day because she was putting on makeup and I asked her, "Why do you put that on your face?" She replied, "I want to make sure I look good for your Dad."

One day after school, we were all outside playing and chasing each other. I was running at top speed and Thomas couldn't slow down without crashing into me, so I skid on the dirt and toppled over, landing on a stick that scraped my thigh. I screamed in agony. Thomas jumped up and ran to my side. "Are you okay Vivi?" He stammered. "No!" I wailed. "It hurts so bad!" Brian hastily ran over and lifted my arm up to help me stand. As I cried out, Thomas held me on my other side and we limped together towards the back door, one step at a time. The red scrape seared and burned as I stepped up inside the house. Shirl came running towards us, through the kitchen, frazzled from my hysteria. She immediately took my hand and guided me to the bathroom to get a better look. She sat down on the edge of the bathtub, then laid me across her lap. She grazed her fingers across my scrape and I cried uncontrollably. "Do you have to put peroxide on it?" I whimpered. "No, baby, I don't have to." Shirl said sweetly. She told me to brace myself as she was about to place a cloth on it. A cool compress coated my thigh and I shook in pain. A chill ran through my body as the compress felt colder and colder. Shirl rubbed my hand, trying to get me to relax. She was no longer frazzled but calm and in control. She knew exactly what she was doing. The coolness slowly eased the pain and I begin to breathe easier. "How is it feeling now?" Shirl asked me. "A little better", I said shakily. She leaned me back up and hugged me. "You should probably stay in and hold this compress on your leg for a while." She told me. I nodded and smiled. I slowly hopped to the couch in the living room and Shirl turned on the T.V. for me to watch. I fell asleep with her rubbing my hair and the pain slowly became a memory.

There was nothing more exciting than celebrating holidays; it was my absolute favorite thing to do! Every holiday was great but Christmas was the best to me. Every year, we bought a tree and decorated it with bulbs of every color. We had shiny red bulbs, gold bulbs with glitter trim and multicolored bulbs with fancy designs on them. Brian and Thomas helped Dad dress the tree with lights. Charity helped Shirl place the bulbs in all the perfect places and I always put the finishing touches on by dazzling each branch with silver tinsel. I made sure not to miss a spot. I loved how the lights hit the tinsel and made the whole tree sparkle even brighter. After we were done, Charity and I sat and stared at the tree, completely mesmerized at all the colors. Dad came and sat beside us, singing along to all the Christmas tunes in his deep baritone voice. He had us laughing until we were holding our stomachs and too tired to walk to our own beds. Every Christmas Eve, we would do our best to stay up as late as possible but we could never make it to see Santa drop our presents off. On Christmas morning, we bolted from our beds into the living room and saw the Christmas tree overflowing with gifts. "It's Christmas! It's Christmas!" Charity and I shouted. Thomas and Brian raced down the hallway to the living room, then stopped abruptly, as soon as they saw all the gifts under the tree. We all looked at each other and then pummeled through the presents in frenzy, looking for our names. Laughter and shouts filled our living room, as Christmas music played in the background. I gathered my gifts one by one and placed them off to the side. I was overwhelmed with excitement just watching everyone open their gifts, I would have burst from happiness if I opened mine at that moment too. I walked over to our green, velvet couch where Dad and Shirl were snuggled up together watching us. Dad lifted me up and sat me on his lap. I hugged him tightly and Shirl leaned in to hug me as well. My tears of joy fell onto Dad's shirt as he held me close. "Aww, don't cry." Shirl said, as she rubbed my back. "You don't have to be sad." she said softly. I looked up at Dad then at Shirl as I wiped my tears. "I'm not sad." I said. "I'm just really happy to have a dad and a mom like you." That Christmas was one of the best memories we had as a family. I thought that things would always be that perfect.

2: "You won this time, but I won't let you win again."

I ran at full speed towards the front porch as soon as we reached my Grandparent's driveway. A gust of wind took my breath away as I was lifted by my Granddad into an embrace and he strained as he lowered me back down to the ground. "Oh, you've grown a bit, I think I might have pulled something." he chuckled. He did this every time I saw him, it was our little thing. I rushed past him to hug my Grandma. She was in the kitchen, wiping down the counters. "What are we gonna do today Grandma?" I asked eagerly. "Whatever you want Viv. Y'all can go outside and ride your skates and play." She announced. I grinned from ear to ear, that was exactly what I wanted to hear. "I'm going to ride my skates!" I shouted, then darted out the back door to the yard. Charity trailed right behind me. She was much faster than I was so she darted ahead of me to grab her skates, then plopped down on the wooden swing to fling her shoes off. She squeezed her feet into her skates as fast as she could, then stuck her tongue out at me as I sat down beside her. I giggled. "You won this time but I won't let you win again." I said in a sassy tone. Charity laughed and jumped up just as I finished pulling up my last skate. She rolled slightly to her right before gaining control and becoming sturdy. It showed on her face that she was still trying to find her balance. I giggled. She kept looking at her wrist, pretending that she was checking the time, as she waited for me to finish lacing up my skates. I looked up at her and puffed out my lips. "I am not slow!" I said as I stood from the bench. "She rolled her neck at me and said, "Slow as time", in my grandmother's voice. I couldn't help but laugh. Charity always imitated people under her breath whenever they said something funny. She mimicked them perfectly and always stood and walked the same way they did. She would puff her chest out and squint her eyes as she pretended to be my cousin Shonie. Her butterscotch skin glowed in the sun as she looked down at me and asked, "Who am I?" I erupted in laughter as she sneered up her nose and wagged her finger at me. I reached my hand out to her as I tried to catch my breath from laughing. My cousin Shonie was always mean to me and would never share her toys whenever we would go to her house. Charity would imitate her and pretend she was melting like the witch in Wizard of Oz. That was my favorite! Charity rolled behind me and put her hands on my shoulders. "Choo, Choo." she yelled out. "Chugga-chugga. Chugga-chugga." I echoed back. We found a perfect rhythm to skate to as we climbed the hill in front of my Grandparent's house. As the hill became steeper, Charity let go of my shoulders and did her best to balance on her own. As we got closer to the top, we anticipated the thrill of going down full speed and slowing down in just enough time to roll into the grass. We skated side by side, reaching our hands out to each other in fear of falling over. We were huffing as we reached the top and gave each other the biggest grin while trying to catch our breath. We swiveled in a circle to face downhill; it was time to be daredevils! We grabbed each other's hand and squealed as we pushed off on our skates. "3-2-1", we shouted. We started rolling downward and instantly picked up speed. I was cheesing from ear to ear as Charity squeezed my hand tighter. She screamed as we zoomed down, the wind deforming our cheeks as our speed increased. I laughed and screamed as the adrenaline rushed through my body. As we neared the bottom, we let go of each other; and zoomed in opposite directions. I rolled into the driveway, doing my best ice skating impersonation of a rounding spin and then tumbled into the grass. "Wow that was so much fun!" Charity exclaimed. "Wanna go again?"

She asked breathlessly. "Yes!" I shouted. We made our

way back up the hill and rode down several times until we

were completely exhausted. I rolled into the grass after

making it down the hill for the last time. I was laughing

uncontrollably at Charity almost toppling over as she came

down. Charity's thick, black hair blew in the wind like the

clothes on the laundry line. As we sped down, it flew right

in her face, masking her eyes. She struggled to move it as it

blew in different directions and she inched closer to the

bottom of the hill. She flapped her hands rapidly around her

face to grab the loose hair and screamed, "I'm gonna

crash!" I grabbed her hand and tilted my skates upward so I

could brake and slow her speed. She swiveled but clung to

my hand as we rolled into the grass. I looked up at her and

she looked like she had been electrocuted. Her face was in

shock and her hair stood up like a rooster. We couldn't help but erupt in laughter together. I had to concentrate on breathing from laughing so hard. I sat down in the grass and looked up at the baby blue sky, covered in clouds. The sun beamed on my skin and I felt like I could sit there all day in the warmth. I smiled at the sun and wiggled my feet out of my skates. I felt like going to jump rope so I leaped up and headed for the backyard. I sang to myself, "Miss Mary Mack, Mack Mack, all dressed in black, black, black with silver buttons, buttons, buttons all down her back, back, back! She asked her mother, mother, mother, for 50 cents, cents, cents!" "Look Vivi!" Charity shouted. "To see the elephant...eleph...I slowly stopped jumping my rope, what is it"? I asked. "It's a cocoon! We learned about them in class." Charity exclaimed. She was leaning against the tallest tree in the backyard. I crept over to her, convinced that I may disturb the caterpillar if I ran. "Look at how layered it is." Charity marveled. The cocoon was so intricate and mysterious. We were both standing there fascinated, looking at the cocoon and then at each other. "I can't wait for the butterfly to come out!" I chanted as I threw my hands in the air. "It's gonna be new and improved and beautiful and colorful and all the things that make it wonderful!" I exclaimed. I spun around in circles giggling until I was dizzy. I plopped down on the swing, squinting up at the sky as the sun was setting. I just loved discovering new things and learning at my grandparents. We always found a way to make an adventure out of the simplest things that we did.

The sun was completely hidden now by the clouds and darkness that had covered the backyard. Suddenly, a flash of light caught my attention a little distance from where I sat. I jumped up immediately. Brian came out the back door and rushed in the direction that I spotted the illumination.

He was so fast! "I got them!" He yelled in triumph as I raced over to him. He opened his cupped hands to reveal three lightning bugs flickering rapidly. He was always the best at catching them. I jumped and squealed and leaped in all directions trying to catch just one, but they would always slip away just before I clamped my hands together. Time sped by as we ran in frenzy around the backyard in competition.

"Y'all come on in and get ready for supper." My Grandma said softly. I looked up at the back door where she stood and smiled, then slowly proceeded towards the stairs behind Charity. I was exhausted and hunger pinged my stomach as the smell of sweet cornbread filled my nostrils. Once inside, I looked at the backyard before closing the door and smiled. The lightning bugs flashed at me brightly, as if they were saying good game; see you next time.

Being at grandma's was one of my favorite places to be. We were always free to have as much fun as we wanted. One night as we all were getting ready for bed, Brian started to tell a story that he made up as he went along. Grandma was arranging the blankets on the pull-out bed in the den to make sure we were extra comfortable. "Y'all gon' head and get in bed." She said to us. She tucked us in, packing blanket after blanket on top of us. She made sure that we would never be cold. The blankets were heavy on my little body so I was completely locked in place. I wiggled and twisted to try and get comfortable, but the blankets did not budge. Charity giggled at me as I shifted in slow motion under the mound. Brian told me to just stop moving and I would be comfortable. "Ok, I whispered. "Tell us some more of the story." I encouraged. "Little Wagon was on an adventure," he began, "Today he was going to the land before time. Little Wagon had his red, corduroy overalls on and his red wagon was packed with his toys and everything that he needed. He walked down the sidewalk in Roseland trying to figure out which way to go. He looked around and noticed some animals trailing behind him. He saw a bunny and a cat that were following along. "Do you guys want to come with me?" Little Wagon asked them. They nodded and jumped in the wagon. He was excited to have some friends coming along with him. He jumped in his wagon and pushed with all his might. The wagon sped down the road, and they were on their way."

"When were they gonna get to the land before time?" I asked Brian eagerly "And what are they gonna do there?" I added "Let's get some sleep Vivi." Brian answered. "I'll tell some more of the story tomorrow." Charity was already snoring beside me. I couldn't believe she fell asleep during the story! I was fascinated by what Little Wagon had planned and where he was headed. I had so many questions for Brian about why he was leaving his home and how he ate and where he went to school. I laid there, mulling over my questions and trying my best to answer them myself. I slowly drifted off to sleep, fading into a deep dream where I found myself walking down that very sidewalk Little Wagon was on. He was in Roseland, but it looked like a brand new place. It was painted in all orange with beautiful flowers everywhere. There was ice cream and cake hanging from the trees and there were cups of lemonade and Hawaiian Punch on the street. I pranced around, so surprised at how everything looked. I heard wheels squeaking and turned to see Little Wagon toting his load at the end of the cul-de-sac. He was walking really slowly, so I caught up to him quickly as I ran. "Little Wagon, Little Wagon, where are you going?" I asked breathlessly. He stopped abruptly and I could see him adjusting his overalls as they were dragging on the sidewalk. I stood in front of him and noticed his bright red hat. His head was down and he didn't move at all. "I was wondering where you were headed." I said excitedly, awaiting his response. He slowly looked up at me and smiled. I stepped back in shock as I seen his face. He looked just like Dad! I opened my mouth to ask him again, where he was headed but nothing came out. Everything faded away and I woke up trying to make sense of what I saw. I didn't realize then, how much that dream would mean to me later.

3: "You're a special girl."

Dad is my number one superhero! He is the best man that I know and every chance that I get to spend with him is amazing! His dark skin always glistens in the sunlight and he looks like someone out of a magazine. He is tall and handsome and his clothes are always so neat and creased. He keeps his hair trimmed low but I can always tell when he gets his hair freshly cut. I light up every time he comes home, and I anticipate sharing all my thoughts with him. He usually has to tell me to slow down when I talk because with all my excitement, everything comes out so quickly and sounds like gibberish. But no matter how I sound, he always understands me.

My favorite outings are when Dad takes us to Freedom Park, where we run and skate around the beautiful pond for hours. It's one of my favorite places to go because I always have so much fun! The last time he took us, we were getting ready to leave and I went to throw some trash away with Charity and Brian. We were laughing and talking as Charity opened the trashcan and just as she pulled the lid up, a squirrel jumped out at us! I screamed and jumped back in shock, as it flew past and landed on the ground. Our feet were stuck in place as we eyed the frightened squirrel, scurry away. We turned back to each other, with our hearts pounding and small smirks appearing on our faces. We instantly burst into laughter, amazed at what just happened. There were always moments like this that made going to the park so memorable.

One day while there, Dad stopped to tell us the name of a tree we never heard of before. It was a Weeping Willow and he told us why it had that name. I thought the tree was beautiful but I could also see how it looked as if it were weeping and sad. Dad always found a way to make a fun lesson out of everything we encountered. He quizzes us on the types of plants or different clouds in the sky that we see. And he also challenges us to come up with new ways to keep the pond clean as sometimes, we see all kinds of cups and food wrappers floating in the water.

Dad usually leaves early in the morning to go to work and comes home at night, eats dinner with us and then goes to bed. On the weekends, he works in the morning and when he gets home, I can tell that he is very tired, but he always insists on taking us to the park. Dad runs with us and picks me up to let me ride on his back. I hold onto him tightly and giggle as I bounce with every step he takes.

Every Sunday night, Dad lets us pick a word out of the dictionary and gives us the week to memorize the definition, then recite it to him. We lovingly referred to our time together as the Word of the Week session. Each time,

I would breeze through my presentation, speaking with conviction when it was my turn to be tested. I always loved to see Dad smile in pride and exclaim that I did an excellent job. He would always say that I was just like him; such a scholar and great with my words. Every Sunday, I looked forward to seeing him and telling him about my week. He didn't have to work on Sundays, so it was our chance to talk with him as much as we wanted. We could ask a million questions, (in which I did), or simply just talk about our feelings. I always told him about a new book I read or what I learned in school that week. I loved to tell him how fascinated I was at the new things I discovered. Then I would tell him if anything was bothering me. When I told him about a problem I was having at school, he would stop me and ask me to label the conflict. A couple weeks before, our word of the week was conflict. I remember being confused about the definition and how Dad explained it. He said that a conflict was always between two things, but I had believed that a conflict could be between multiple things. He continued to remind me that a conflict can have multiple factors that create it but it is between two opposing forces. So, whenever I presented a problem to him, we would label the factors and we would come up with a solution to the problem together. "What are the opposing forces?" Dad would ask. "There are two." I would answer. Then he would give me a high five and say, "You're super smart!" I would beam with pride.

I would always hear him in my head as I raised my hand to answer questions at school. "You're super smart Vivi Dove! You are a smart girl!"

School was my favorite place to be, besides being at home. I excelled tremendously in my classes and won the award three times in a row for the most books read for my class.

My teacher took a special interest in me and told me often how advanced I was to be in the 2nd grade. She had me read things aloud to the class or give a summary of what a book was about and I gladly stood up and read for my class. "You're a special girl." She would say to me. "Thank you", I would reply, with the biggest grin on my face.

A month before summer break began, Dad got a new job working for an insurance company that required him to work early hours and weekends as well. He told us that he would have to work very late some days but he would still have some weekends that we could spend time together. He promised to take us to Freedom Park on the weekends he had off. He took us out that day for ice cream to celebrate his new position and we were delighted. I didn't understand what Dad did, I just knew he was very good at it, that's why they wanted him to work so much. Months had gone by and summertime had arrived. We were out of school and excited about all the fun things we would do. Shirl spent the first week packing food each day to take to the park and eat. She spread out a blanket right in front of the pond so we could watch the ducks swim. She made us bologna sandwiches and we had fruit and crackers to snack on before jetting right back out to ride our skates. A few weeks later, Dad was off and he took us to Carowinds. It was the most fun we ever had! We rode ride after ride, ate funnel cakes, drank Pepsi and even won a big teddy bear, playing a game in the arcade. As we drove back home in our station wagon, I looked out the window to catch a glimpse of the roller coasters one more time. The sun was setting and we all were completely exhausted. Charity was already asleep on my shoulder. I looked over to see Brian and Thomas asleep as well and thought about how scared they were on the rides; it was hilarious! Dad noticed that I was still up and reached back to me from the passenger seat and grabbed my hand. I held it tightly, smiling as he whispered, "Love you Vivi Dove." I looked back out of the window and slowly faded off to sleep. I never felt as safe as I did at that moment, riding back from Carowinds.

4: "I heard your loud voice."

A new school year began and I was excited about being a 3rd grader. I had a new teacher by the name of Ms. Byrd who was delighted to have me in her class, as she told Dad and Shirl at the open house. Dad had just gotten off work in enough time for us to make it to the open house social where they had ice cream and all kinds of snacks for the families that attended. Ms. Byrd gave me a bag full of stickers and worksheets to take home. I was so anxious to work on them, I pulled them out as soon as we got in the car. "Look at this Charity! Isn't it so cool?" I beamed. "I love all my stuff from my new teacher!" I said to Dad. "I'm glad you do Vivi Dove, you're going to do great in her class!" he added. Shirl was unusually quiet on the ride back home and didn't seem very happy. "Mom, are you ok? I asked thoughtfully. She didn't say anything back to me and continued to stare out the passenger window. Dad was driving and had Phil Collins playing so I thought she may not have heard me. "Mom", I said loudly. Shirl quickly turned around and shouted, "Close your mouth now, you are too loud!" I jumped back in complete shock. "She is always talking and making noise." She snapped over at Dad as if I couldn't hear her. "You don't have to yell at her Shirl." Dad retorted.

I didn't know what I did wrong, I just wanted to make sure she was ok. My eyes filled up with tears as I looked over at Charity. Her eyes were wide in shock along with Thomas and Brian. None of us had ever heard her yell like that. Once we got home, I steered clear by looking at my stickers in my room to make sure not to upset her again. That night as we laid down in our beds, we heard Dad and Shirl arguing for the first time in their room. Shirl was yelling about Dad lying and not coming home on time. I didn't understand why she said that because Dad doesn't lie, he always keeps his promises.

I struggled to fall asleep that night, tossing back and forth with my body and the thoughts in my mind. Hearing Dad and Shirl argue was something I never thought would happen, but this was the start of many restless nights. As time went on, I noticed a change in Shirl's temper and the way she acted towards us. I also noticed that she wasn't putting on makeup anymore, like she used to. She would put it on sometimes on the weekends, but it became less and less that I saw her do it. She would drag around the house in her pajamas and lay on the couch watching TV when we got home from school. I still looked forward to popsicles after getting off the bus but Shirl no longer greeted us with them. Instead, Shirl started making us clean up the house after completing our homework. She would just lay motionless on the couch, randomly shouting at us to hurry up and clean faster. We were always in trouble but it seemed that I was the one that got punished for things whenever she was upset. "I heard your loud voice." She would say as she would point at me. One time Charity told a joke and we were all kicking and laughing on the floor. We were holding our bellies as we laughed together, trying to catch our breath. Shirl stormed in our room and smacked me so hard in my mouth, my cheeks swelled up. "Shut that loud mouth!" She shouted. I screamed out at her and she threatened to smack me again if I didn't quiet down. It made no sense why she hit me when I wasn't the only one laughing. Charity and Brian came to comfort me as soon as she left the room but I brushed them away. I didn't want their hugs, I just wanted to cry alone.

Brian's birthday had come around and we were all so excited about the festivities we would have after school. Dad always bought us the best presents and a nice cake when it was our birthday. We were all in the kitchen after dinner, excited for Dad to be home and awaiting our plate of ice-cream and cake. Shirl was a completely different person. She had her makeup done beautifully and her jet-black hair was curled all over. She wore a light blue top that had frills at the end and she smiled at us like she hadn't seen us in years. Shirl announced, "We got you your favorite cake Brian; coconut cake!" He cheesed from ear to ear. Everyone got quiet as he prepared to blow out his candles and make a wish. "What are you gonna wish for?" Thomas asked. We all burst out in laughter. "He can't tell you silly!" Charity retorted. I laughed loudly, shaking my head at Thomas. "Happy Birthday to you, Happy Birthday to you!" We all sang harmoniously. Brian's beautiful, dark skin was illuminated by the candles on the cake and his smile lit up the room even brighter. He blew with all his might and the candles were out! We clapped and cheered loudly. Shirl began cutting the cake and placing them on plates. She passed them out one by one and smiled sweetly. She cut another piece and placed it on a plate with ice-cream and handed it to me. I smiled back and said timidly, "Mom, I don't like coconut, it's nasty." I waited for her understanding reply but instead, Shirl instantly gripped my arm and yanked me out of the kitchen, making me drop my plate on the floor. She marched toward the room and swung around; looking down at me. "Since you don't like coconut, little girl, you can go to bed." She snarled. I stared at her shaken up and confused. "But I don't want to go to bed, I want to have ice cream." I wailed. She gripped my arm even tighter and I screamed out, "You're hurting me", hoping Dad would hear me. She then flung me onto the bed and released my arm. "Good!" she shouted, then slammed the door. I sobbed into my hands as I sat on my bed. I was so hurt and couldn't believe how mean Shirl was being. It was dark in the room and I heard everyone laughing in the kitchen. I just wanted to be in there with everyone and not by myself. Just then, the bedroom door slowly opened and Dad walked in. "Come on Vivi Dove, and get some ice-cream." He said cheerfully. I looked at him tearfully and jumped up to run to his side. "Thank you, Dad!" I said happily. "Dad can I tell you something?" I asked. "Sure Vivi", he said as he bent down to look at me. "Mom always hurts us. She is mean to all of us when you're not here. She hits Brian, Charity and I but only yells at Thomas and she is not a good person! She makes me cry and she…, Dad put his hand on my shoulder to calm me. "Vivi, are you doing what she says?" He asked. I nodded my head quickly, then blurted out, "We always do! I'm a good girl and I listen." I said. "I know, Vivi Dove", Dad said while rubbing my arm. You keep being the good girl that you are and things will get better. I promise."

Even though Dad promised that things would get better, they didn't. Shirl stopped allowing us to play outside with our friends after school and the only time we were able to watch TV was when Dad was home. On Saturday mornings, we would get up early and grab a bowl of cereal to watch our morning cartoons. Dad stayed in the room with Shirl and her mood was always better on the weekends. It was a relief when Dad had the entire weekend off because he would cook for everyone and it was the one thing that would lighten Shirl's mood and guarantee that she was back to her old self. I would love the moments where we started to feel like a family again, it was what I missed most. One Sunday evening after a great weekend that Dad was off, Thomas, Brian, Charity and I were getting our things ready for school the next morning. We did our Word of the Week with Dad and then he went back in the room with Shirl. We all dreaded Monday because Dad would be back at work and we wouldn't have any fun until the next time we saw him. We had hopes that Shirl's good mood would last throughout the week but it never did. We were all in our room talking and laughing when Dad appeared in the hallway with Shirl. "We have a surprise for you bean heads! He said with a grin. I jumped up and raised my hand. "Can I guess?" I squealed. "Go for it Vivi Dove!" Dad said. "I think the surprise is, we get to go skating tomorrow after school!" I said enthusiastically. "That's not it Vivi, but you still can go skating." Dad said. My eyes widened as I looked back at my siblings and we all grinned from ear to ear. I smiled as I looked over at

Shirl and her expression told me that I shouldn't even think about touching my skates the next day. I put my head down as I sat, hoping that Dad would remind her about skating, in case she told us no.

"Any more guesses?" Dad probed. We all shook our heads. He slowly got down on his knees and started to rub Shirl's stomach. He looked at her and then looked at us. "She's pregnant guys! We're having a baby!" Dad beamed.

5: "...Trying to teach him the right word."

A new baby, I couldn't believe it! I was excited because I loved babies and I wanted to be able to help with the baby when he or she was born. I asked Charity that night what she thought it might be. "I hope it's a girl!" She said happily. "Well I hope it's a boy and a girl! I whispered. "What if it's twins? That would be so cool!" I added. Charity had already fallen asleep but I stayed up thinking of the new baby and how it could bring the family together again. I thought about my friends at school and how they had new brothers and sisters and how excited they were to tell Ms. Byrd. I always said they were so lucky to have a baby brother or sister because they could teach them everything they know. One day after school, we all resumed our usual chores without being told. Shirl was spread out on the couch, snoring so we tiptoed past her to avoid waking her up. I cleaned the bathroom and finished in record time. I decided to help since I was done so quickly so I went into the room to help Thomas finish dusting. As I began dusting, I asked Thomas, "What did you do in class today?" This year, we had different teachers. He smiled and said, "We got to go to the lie-berry and pick out books and look at magazines." "You mean library", I said slowly. Thomas scrunched his face up and said, "No it's lie-berry." "No, it's not", I whispered, completely halting my dusting. It's l-i-b-r-a-r-y, which spells library!" I concluded. Thomas instantly threw his dust rag down and jetted to the living room. I heard him waking Shirl up and telling her that I was correcting him and telling him the wrong word. I stood completely still, shaking inside and hoping she didn't pay him any mind. She slowly approached from the hallway and entered the room. I backed into the wall as she came closer and I shielded myself in fear of the first blow she would throw. "Get in my room now!" She blared. Tears started falling from my eyes. I knew she was going to make me take my clothes off before spanking me. "Please", I begged. I was just trying to teach him the right word." I scurried across the room and headed out the door, knowing that if I continued begging, she would beat me longer. She slammed the door behind her and told me to strip. I shook in fear as I took off my clothes, then stood completely naked. She flung the belt strap across my legs and I buckled as the sting shocked my skin. She flung it back again, hitting the same spot and I cried out. "I was just trying to teach him the right word!"

"You think you're so smart!" She shouted. She whipped me with the belt across my back. The sharp sting knocked me to the ground and I stumbled on my knees, trying to regain my composure but I couldn't. The belt just kept coming and coming, lash after lash until I couldn't cry out anymore. Shirl didn't care where the belt landed, she just kept striking me. With each lash, she bore down harder and harder, making sure I felt her rage. My body convulsed as I had no control of my movements and all I could do was pray that she would stop. I mustered up enough energy to put my hands up to block her lashes from the front of me. My mouth opened but I couldn't say anything as each swing of the belt took my breath away. I looked at Shirl's face and could see that she hated me and she wasn't going to stop. She struck down again so forcefully that she flung the belt out of her hand and the buckle knocked across my head, slashing my forehead with the sharp end. Blood started to run onto the floor. I knew something was wrong, I just couldn't move, my body was paralyzed in pain. Shirl reached out for my hand and pulled me off the floor. My legs wobbled like a newborn giraffe trying to find its balance. I could barely support myself as she lifted me up from under my arms. She placed me on her bed and left quickly out of the room. She returned with a large, wet cloth and positioned it on the front of my head where I felt the blood dripping from. Sit up straight, she growled. I tried to adjust my posture but had no energy left in me. I slumped over, looking down at the red stain on the carpet where my head laid. "Am I going to die?" I thought. I felt like my body had fallen off a building and my head throbbed like I landed head first. I could barely keep my eyes open as I faded in and out of consciousness. Shirl had dressed me and was carrying me to my room. All I remember is waking up in my bed and Shirl seated beside me, moving the wet towel on my head. I faded back to sleep and upon waking up again, I noticed that it was light outside. I sat up, knowing that I had missed my bus and was going to get in trouble for it. I stumbled as I stood and looked down at my legs. There were red and purple welts all over my thighs and I noticed them on my arms as well. It instantly came back to me, what happened the night before. I reached up to feel my head and there was a small cloth covering the throbbing spot. I had a scarf wrapped around my head, holding the cloth in place. I looked up and Shirl was standing in the doorway. My heart pounded and I tensed up. "Do you want some breakfast?" She asked in a strained high pitch. I was afraid to answer. "Come and have some breakfast and you can watch some TV", she continued. She could tell my confusion and mistrust as I continued to stand there, unsure of what was going on. "I thought that you should stay home today and just relax." You can go back to school tomorrow." She said, as she came closer and rubbed my back. I nodded and walked slowly with her to the kitchen. I spent all day watching my favorite shows and eating food and snacks that Shirl prepared. Despite my soreness, I was happy that she was being nice to me. I fell asleep on the couch and was awakened by the sound of screeching wheels from the school bus outside. "They're home!" I thought to myself, lacking the energy to jump up in joy. I looked up and Shirl was there, looking around on the floor. She grabbed my dolls and flung them in the direction of my room. She instantly snatched the scarf off my head and grabbed the blood-soaked towel that flopped to the floor. She shut the TV off and looked at me. "Get up, and go do your chores." She growled. I heard Charity, Brian and Thomas coming through the door and I knew my good time had come to an end. I limped towards the bathroom, holding my throbbing head.

6: *"Things will get better soon."*

"Abandon: To give up completely, (a course of action, a practice, or a way of thinking.)

Cease to support or look after someone, to desert." I whispered the definition as I lay motionless on my bed, peering into darkness. Abandon was our word of the week. I'd memorized the definition and anxiously awaited a chance to share it with Dad, but Shirl sent us to bed early and I couldn't figure out why.

I attempted to say something to her about it but Brian grabbed me before I could knock on her door. I yanked away from him in protest. "She must have forgotten, I just wanted to remind her." I whispered to him. "That's not a good idea Vivi." Brian whispered back as he pointed to my forehead. We hadn't been home very long from Grandma's before she ushered us to take our baths. "Get in there and wash up!" she ordered. Everything was a demand with her.

We simply did what she said and didn't ask any questions. I wondered if Thomas was being a tattle tale again and told Shirl that I said he wasn't my real brother. While we were at Grandma's, I told him that I never wanted to play with him again. He kept saying that he was sorry and that he didn't' know I was going to get hurt by Shirl. I didn't believe him so Charity and I pinky swore not to play with him anymore.

"Maybe the baby inside of her is making her evil", Charity said. "Ever since Dad told us she was pregnant, she has been so mean to us! One thing is for sure though," she added, I really hope that baby doesn't come out like her."

"I hope she is nice and sweet like Grandma." Thomas chimed in. We all ignored him.

My heart stampeded when I heard the lock on the front door click, Dad was home! I shifted slightly, making sure not to rumble the plastic covering on my bed. I listened intently for his baritone voice. "Where are the kids?" He asked. I beamed, glad that I wasn't the only one who found it odd for us to be in bed so early. "They were acting like animals, misbehaving, so I sent them to bed." Shirl said. I gasped. "What!" I mouthed in shock." I waited for Dad's response but nothing came. My eyes darted back and forth in the darkness, desperate to hear him retort. Then I heard footsteps nearing the hallway that trailed to their bedroom. The door shut loudly and echoed for a few minutes, then silence. I shook my head in disbelief. "She lied to him! We didn't do anything!" I thought to myself. I sat up in protest, my face scrunched up in anger. She knew how important it was to for us to see him on Sundays. Dad coming home was always the highlight of our evening. Every once in a while, when he would get off earlier during the week, we were able to talk to him before venturing to bed. He would always squat down and put his hand on my shoulder, and ask, "How you doing Vivi Dove?" Before I could answer, I would always feel Shirl come up behind me and I would instantly freeze up. I had developed a severe stutter due to my fear of Shirl, so every time I spoke in front of her, I could never speak a complete sentence. She would look down at me and smile, daring me to tell him how she treats us. But all I could ever muster was "I'm doing well" as my reply to Dad. Shirl would rub my arm as she walked away in satisfaction. I always wondered if Dad was so complimentary towards me during Word of the Week because I never spoke properly whenever he was home. Whenever he would take me in the privacy of their room, I still stuttered in fear of Shirl overhearing me.

"I'm gonna talk to her about it, ok." He would say, after I told him about how Shirl hits us. "Just make sure you listen and stay out of her way." He would add.

"Why do you have to work so much?" I would ask – then plead with him by adding, "Can you be here with us more?" His reply would always be, "It'll get better Vivi Dove, things will get better soon."

I slowly leaned back onto my pillow, feeling completely defeated. My talks with Dad were the only thing that really kept me going because living with Shirl had become a nightmare. Our talks were the only thing that gave me hope that things would one day get better. But as I lay there, my fears deepened for what Shirl was capable of. Without our talks, I knew that things were only going to get worse.

7: *"You should have listened to her."*

Weeks had gone by without speaking with Dad. During the week, Shirl would have us cleaning the house from top to bottom after school, so we were completely drained when it was time for bed. On a couple nights, I would hear Dad open our door and peek in the room then shut it back quietly. On those nights, I wanted so badly to let him know I was still awake but the words just wouldn't come out. It became a habit of mine to stay up until I heard him come home. I would be comforted by hearing his voice but would end up crying myself to sleep, feeling completely alone. Shirl found out that I was staying up later to hear Dad at night. I was constantly falling asleep in class and Ms. Byrd's assistant sent a friendly note home stating: "Make sure Vivian is getting an adequate amount of sleep, so she's able to participate in class." On Sundays, Shirl found pleasure in sending us to bed early without dinner. She would always say, "I need to make sure you get adequate sleep and that leaves no time for you to eat." It was her sick little game she would play with us. She would cook a big meal and upon arrival home from Grandma's, we would be excited to have dinner together. She would shoo us away saying, "Go wait in your room until I'm done and ready for ya'll to come eat." We would talk quietly and make up little games until it was time for dinner. She would later come into our room and we would sit up straight as she stood in front of us. "I changed my mind, get ready for bed." She would snap. "Ya'll don't deserve anything to eat tonight." Our disappointment clearly shown on our faces and she would smile in satisfaction. "Why did she insist on making us so sad?" I would wonder. I didn't understand why she hated us so much.

One night, Shirl kept me up to finish my hair for picture day the next morning. I could barely keep my eyes open, it was so late. I sat completely still as she twisted each strand of hair. My arms laid across her thighs as I sat on the thin carpet floor in the middle of her legs. The throbbing from my freshly pulled ponytails kept me alert enough to know she was close to finishing. She pulled the last portion of loose hair into a tight twist then wrapped it with a rubber band. I cringed as she pulled the hair together tighter, making the corners of my eyes slant diagonally. Every time she did my hair, I got a face lift to go with it as well. Shirl nudged my head, signaling that she was finished. I slowly stood up and stretched my arms in the air then yawned. I bent down to gather the comb and brush off the floor and as I did, the front door opened. In walked my hero, tired and worn out from a long day at work. I stood there beaming as he came to embrace me in a hug. "Hey Vivi Dove, he said. "Hi Dad!" I exclaimed with the last bit of energy I had. "Go on and head to bed so you can get some rest", he told me, then kissed me on my forehead. I said goodnight then turned to look at Shirl's face; she grimaced as I walked to my room grinning from ear to ear.

The next morning, before leaving to catch the bus, Shirl yanked me by the arm and said in a staccato like rhythm, "Don't. Touch. Your. Hair!" I nodded my head robotically. She shook my arm and tightened her grip. "What do you say?" She pressed. "Yes Ma'am." I stuttered. She slowly loosened her grasp on me as the bus neared our cul-de-sac. She stood up and walked back towards our front door without saying goodbye.

My head bobbed up and down as I struggled to stay awake on our way to school. I wanted to lean my head against the window but my head was throbbing from the barrettes clamped against my scalp. Shirl's words turned over and over in my head like a broken record. "Don't touch your hair." My head continued to throb profusely.

"No smiles for me this morning?" Ms. Byrd teased as I sat down on our thinking rug beside my classmates. "Are we all ready for Picture Day?" She asked the class. Cheers and yells filled the room as my classmates bounced up and down on the rug in excitement. I painted on a fake smile to try and fit in but I knew Ms. Byrd saw through it. We all stood up and formed a line to prepare to go down the hallway towards the library. Ms. Byrd stopped beside me and winked. "My hair bows are too tight and it hurts really bad." I whispered desperately to her. "Let me try and loosen them before we head there." She said sweetly. One by one, she loosened the barrettes and I felt like heaven had lifted me up. I let out a sigh of relief at the sudden cease of agony caused from the barrettes. I was so grateful for her that day. I smiled really big for my pictures and completely forgot about my hair for the rest of my day. After arriving home, I set my bookbag down near the kitchen table then rushed in the living room where Charity and Brian were sitting. "Look what I learned today." I said while giggling. I kicked straight in the air then jabbed around me like a martial artist. "Hiyah!" I said as I formed a fighting stance. Charity cackled at my little show. "You're really good." Brian added. I grinned as I spun around in a circle then instantly jumped back and let out a scream. Shirl had been standing directly behind me. She immediately charged at me, yanked my arm and slammed me up against the wall. The force knocked the breath out of me. My eyes were wide open in shock and my heart pounded like a drum. Shirl peered into me and asked, "What did I tell you about messing with your hair?" I looked back at her and didn't know what to say. I believe that my silence infuriated her more. She shoved her hand around my neck and lifted me up on the wall. She pinned me there like a poster, tightening her grip around my neck. My legs dangled below like a ragdoll.

"What did I tell you about messing with your hair?" She growled.

I wasn't sure if she was expecting me to answer, but there was no way that I could utter a word. I helplessly looked down at Brian and Charity below as I tried to take short breaths but got no relief. I looked to my right and saw Thomas doing his homework as if nothing was happening. I started to panic, realizing that I couldn't breathe. I squirmed as Shirl continued to choke me, pressing more force on my neck than before. I knew she wanted me to die and this was her chance to make it happen. Tears streamed down my face and I flailed my arms helplessly in protest.

"STOP, PLEASE STOP!" Charity begged. "She can't breathe!" I felt dizzy and I lost focus of Shirl's face, it was distorted and blurry. My stomach felt like it would burst from no oxygen and then I felt my body give up. At that moment, Shirl instantly dropped me and I plummeted to the floor. I collapsed on my knees and the thud shook my entire body. I cried hysterically as I inhaled gulps of air. Shirl was yelling something that I couldn't make out. Her voice trailed down the hallway into her room. I stayed right there in the spot she left me, still gasping for air. Charity rubbed my back slowly, whimpering in tears. I looked up to see Brian crying and it broke my heart. I felt so broken and completely defenseless. I had to tell Dad.

I refused to fall asleep until Dad came home that night, so I could tell him about what she had done. The front door shut and I jumped up to make sure that I went through with my plan. I needed to head to the bathroom in order for Dad to know I was still awake and find a way to talk to him. I opened my room door slowly and counted the minutes I needed to be in the hallway to meet them on the way to their room. I was trembling. I heard them approaching and I scurried to reach the bathroom just in time for Dad to notice. He saw me and walked towards the door. Shirl was right behind him as I predicted and I struggled to open my mouth. He noticed the distraught look on my face and asked, "What's wrong Vivi Dove?" I had practiced what I planned to say, over and over but I was so overwhelmed with emotion that I couldn't keep myself together. I whelped into his arms. My body convulsed as I cried out loud, unable to speak. He put his arms around me and I wept even harder. "She's so dramatic." I heard Shirl sneer behind him. "She does this because you give her a stage to do it", she barked at him. He leaned back so that I could gather myself and he asked again, what was wrong. I looked up at Shirl as I began to speak. Pushing as hard as I could to just say the words I wanted but I couldn't. I stuttered tremendously, shaking as I spoke. Ca… ca… ca…

It took me 5 minutes to just say "can". I felt pathetic as Shirl grinned down at me. Dad pulled a notepad from his pocket and handed me a pen. I exhaled in relief, then wrote: Can I talk to you by myself? He looked down at the pad and nodded, then stood up and whispered to Shirl. I was unsure of what he told her but I awaited her shouts of protest. Surprisingly, she turned around without a word. Dad closed the door behind him then stared intently at me waiting for me to speak. "Dad, I began. Shirl cho… cho… choked me today. I couldn't breathe." He blinked several times before responding as if he were contemplating how he would deal with Shirl.

"What did I tell you to do?" He said. I squinted my watery eyes trying to understand his question. I didn't understand what he was saying.

"What was it that I told you to do?" He persisted. My stuttering continued. "To listen." I said shyly.

"And did you?" Dad pressed.

"No, I whimpered. But...I, I on... only touched my hair be..be... because, it hurt." I dropped my eyes to the floor, feeling ashamed. I never wanted him to be disappointed in me. He put my hands in his and said softly, "You should have listened to her."

I stood there in utter disbelief at what I heard. I looked up at him but didn't know what to say and I couldn't bring myself to even speak. He rubbed my hands as if to bring me comfort. I dropped them to my side, no longer comforted by his touch. I stood there, mouth dry, staring at him and waiting for more of an explanation. I was waiting for him to stand up and march out of the room, fired up and ready to tell Shirl it was over, but he just continued to stare back at me. I couldn't comprehend why I felt guilty and could no longer look him in the eyes but I knew that all my hopes of a hero died at that very moment. I looked back down at the tiled floor, my eyes welling up with tears. He

got up and walked out of the bathroom, abandoning me. I

sat on the edge of the tub, overwhelmed with emotion. All I

could do was rock back and forth holding my chest. My

heart felt like it would fall out. I looked up to see Brian in

front of me. He took my hand and walked me back to the

room to lay down. He rubbed my hair as I whimpered into

my pillow. He whispered to me, "It's ok Vivi, I Love you."

8: "What do you want?"

Summer never represented freedom and fun for us.
Summer meant going days without eating and watching
other kids play outside while doing our best to stay quiet
and invisible.

It was a beautiful, sunny day and Charity, Brian and I sat in
our room looking outside at our friends eating popsicles
and playing jump rope. We wished that we could swap
places with them for just an hour. Our visits to grandma's
had stopped and we hadn't had a chance to have fun in
months. I was missing my skates as well as the constant
laps Charity and I would take going up the hill and back
down. I knew it had something to do with Social Services
investigating us. Before leaving school, Ms. Byrd took me
to the office and had me speak with a social worker. The
school nurse and some of the office staff were in there too.
The school nurse had kept notes of every injury I had over

the past year and decided to report it to the police. I overheard Shirl on the phone, saying she hated the Jones family for calling DSS on her for no reason. I guess she thought Grandma called them and that's why she told us we could no longer go there. I was just glad she didn't find out it was me that told. The last time we were at Grandma's, I finally had a chance to tell her everything that Shirl was doing to us and about the choking incident. I remember telling her that Dad didn't do anything about it. She fussed for about five minutes and then told me that I shouldn't question what Dad does. She said I was getting to be too grown. That was the last time I told Grandma anything.

Before leaving for Summer break, Ms. Byrd asked what love means to me. I looked at her and said, "Love is when you tell someone that they are important and encourage them to do their best. Love is when you stand up for someone even when you are afraid and love is doing everything that you can to make sure someone that you love is safe." Ms. Byrd hugged me tightly; she sniffled and rocked me from side to side. I could tell she was crying. She held me just long enough for me to carry her scent to my memory so I could think back on this moment. "I'll see you in a few months smart girl." I nodded with a smile. She stood up, wiping her tears away, then held my hand until my bus came. I'll never forget looking out the window at her as we drove away and how she mouthed the words, "I Love You." I replayed those moments of hugging Ms. Byrd over and over again in my head all summer. It was the only thing that kept me from breaking down. As I became distant with Dad, his presence no longer excited me. He would bend down to hug me with a smile and ask how my day was. I started to wonder if he was taunting me as he knew of the constant abuse I had endured while he was at work. I started to believe that he was on Shirl's side and everyone else for that matter.

Shirl knocked on our open door and we all jumped in shock; turning around to face her. "If you want to go outside, you can." She said softly. I wasn't sure if I heard her correctly so I sat there, not moving a limb. "Go ahead if you'd like." She chimed. Brian stood up first and moved towards the door. He looked back for us to follow and grabbed a hold of our hands. Once we reached the screen door, we bolted out into the playground in disbelief. I couldn't believe she was letting us play! I almost wanted to cry, I was so happy. Maybe she might start being nicer to us, I thought, then ran towards the swings. My feet pushed through the air as I climbed higher and higher with each bolt of my swing. The wind brushed across my face and I closed my eyes at the perfect sensation. Charity tried to push her swing as high as mine but she couldn't. I imitated an evil witch's laughter as I swung back and forth beside her. "Keep going, I'm going to reach the moon!" I yelled to her. Brian swung perfectly on the monkey bars, keeping his grip each time he moved to the next bar. He was so good at that! I would always slip halfway across, unable to hold my weight. But I would always run back around to try it again. The sun felt glorious on my skin as I slowed my swing to a stop. I sat there, looking up at the sky as I usually did. I was daydreaming about the future and how I wanted to fly across the world.

Time swiftly passed and the sun began to beat down relentlessly. I was pouring sweat after racing back and forth down the sidewalk with Charity. I bent over with my hands on my knees and said, "I need some water, I'm thirsty." "Me too", Charity chimed back breathlessly. Brian said he had to use the bathroom, so we headed for the back door to all go in together. I pulled at the screen door but it was locked. Brian tapped on the side of it to get Shirl's attention. She must have forgotten that she locked it. We saw her walk through the kitchen towards us. As she reached for the doorknob to the screen, we all prepared ourselves to go inside. "What do you want?" She sneered. "We wanted to come in and get some water, and I need to use the bathroom." Brian stated. Oh, well that's too bad, Shirl chanted back. You made a decision to go outside, so outside is where you'll stay. "But when can we come in?" I asked. "When it's time to go to bed." She snapped, then slammed the back door in our face. We stood there in shock, exhausted and thirsty. We turned around to face the playground, searching for shade but there was none. Charity kicked at the dirt near our door. "We have to stay out here all day?" She asked. We all were silent. "What are we gonna do about the bathroom? I can't hold it." Brian added. I looked around but didn't see anyone we could ask.

Even if we got in trouble for going to someone else's

house, it was worth it. I thought maybe he could duck down

somewhere without being noticed but there was nowhere

that he could go. Charity and I continued to walk the

grounds but it was of no use. Brian couldn't hold it any

longer so he leaned against the brick building, squatted and

began to relieve himself. I turned away, feeling ashamed

and embarrassed for him. He had no way of cleaning

himself after defecating or any way of getting rid of the

waste. Shirl had reduced our existence to animals. My

clothes were drenched in sweat and I started to gag from

the dryness of my mouth. Hours had gone by and I no

longer could force myself to sit on the swings or pretend

that our time outside was enjoyable. I found a spot in the

grass away from the playground where we would play

duck, duck, goose, and I sat. My stomach growled angrily

as we weren't given dinner the night before and hadn't eaten all day. I was tired of Shirl's sick games. I sat and fantasized about seeing Dad's car drive up and him coming up to the playground to take us away from there forever. I smiled at the thought of him being in a cape, holding all of us in his arms and walking away with ease. I then shook my head in shame for even considering that it was possible. He was the last person that would come. He always told me whenever we would have our talks, that things would get better. He was a liar. As Dad and Shirl's arguments became more frequent, Dad stayed away longer and longer each time. We would see him leaving with a big bag of clothes and a forced smile on his face as if he were headed on an adventure. He was Little Wagon; the only difference was he never invited us to go with him. Whenever he returned, he would laugh and tell jokes with Shirl as if we were the perfect family. I sometimes believed that if we were gone, he wouldn't even notice. Why was I thinking about a hero in a cape? Dad couldn't save us because he needed saving himself.

I thought about our grandparents as I sat there in the grass and I wondered why they never came to see us in Roseland. They knew how Shirl treated us but they never came to visit or relieve us of her hateful games. I remember telling my Aunt Vivian how Shirl had choked me. She came to the house a couple days later and threatened Shirl with a bat. I was so relieved to see her. I thought maybe she would take us with her but she left shortly after cussing Shirl out, and promised to come back and "beat her tail", if she heard anything else.   Shirl was fuming with anger and embarrassment. That night she made me take off all my clothes and she beat me with a switch until I had permanent scars on my body. I decided not to mention it to anyone.

But I wondered why Aunt Vivian never came back to check on us. After months of not seeing them, I just knew that our family would miss us. I just knew that they would rescue us and tell us that we could stay with them, but it never happened. I sat there sweating profusely and exhausted from the heat, trying to think of anyone who could help us. I started to realize that no one cared and that they were all just as guilty as Shirl. Everyone knew what was going on but no one said anything. I guess it was easier to not do anything about it and just hope that it went away.

I went to sit beside Charity and Brian against the brick wall beside the back door. Darkness had covered the sky and I had a feeling that Shirl had forgotten about us. It wouldn't surprise me because she had everything that she loved in the house with her. She had her TV, her food, her golden child Thomas and her soon to be born baby, so that was all that she needed. She never loved us and she never would.

Summertime ended with Dad regaining his backbone and demanding that we be able to go to Grandma's and visit. He took us over there for the weekend and I was somewhat relieved to go. Our trips there, had officially resumed and we were able to have a little fun again. The hard part for me was seeing how Grandma and Grandad continued to pack us in the car and take us back to that dreadful place to live with Shirl. I hated them for it. I was becoming more and more dramatic each time we would have to head back to Roseland. I found something wrong with my knees, or I asked if they could do my hair for school, just to be able to stay there longer. I thought of everything to stall but it never worked. I wonder if I took off my shirt and shorts to reveal all the scars Shirl created, just maybe they would change their mind and keep us. But I guess because they didn't see any scars on my face, they figured I was making it all up. Dad would tell Grandma about things that we did wrong and how he popped us for it. She would say that's good, but she would never ask him about why Shirl beat us hours before he got home for the same thing. I started to despise them. I thought family was supposed to be protecting and that nothing would keep you from shielding the people you love from harm. But they did none of that.

I started to believe all the things Shirl screamed at us. She would say that no one wanted us and that we were a burden to the family. She called us bad kids and said, it was the reason that our grandparents never wanted us to stay past the weekend. I started to look at everyone around me as weak and scared. I saw that they were too intimidated to stand up to the evil witch so I no longer desired to go to Grandma's house. My feelings were all over the place. I told Dad one weekend that I wanted to stay home and not go there. He told me I was being disrespectful and beat me with the belt before throwing me in the car to head there.

To put on for Grandma, he pulled his belt out again after

we arrived, and beat me so that she knew he was the man of

the house. I ran out of tears for the pain I felt.

I thought at one point that I could have made this all up in

my imagination. Ms. Byrd always told me how creative I

was and that I was good at telling stories. Did that mean

that I was a liar too? It couldn't be, because Ms. Byrd

believed me. I think Grandma believed that I was making

things up but I knew I wasn't. My family just believed that

there was no need to discuss what took place in Roseland

because what happens in the house was supposed to stay

there.

9: "And although it's been said, many times, many ways…"

Christmas has always been my favorite holiday. I always loved to see the sparkling lights that hung from every street sign and covered the department stores. It was something about the feeling of Christmas that would just put people in a great mood. Shirl was walking around the house humming to Christmas carols and tunes on the radio. She put up the Christmas tree on her own and wrapped a few gifts to set under it. I noticed that she put on makeup and rouged her lips with a red lipstick. I watched her as she peeked outside the window then back to the wrapping paper on her lap. I quickly peered down at the floor, hoping she hadn't noticed me staring. She smiled and looked at me like I've never seen her do before. I saw gentleness in her smile and a warmth that welcomed me to come closer. She reached out her arms and embraced me in a hug. She pulled back and asked, "Are you full?" I nodded and smiled, doing

my best not to cry. She made a nice dinner for us to eat and

spoiled us with ice cream for dessert. I cleaned my plate,

unsure of the next time we would get a meal like that. I sat

back down on the floor nervously, wondering how long her

niceness would last. The lock on the door clicked and I

looked up to see Dad walk in. He managed to get off early

to take us to see the Christmas lights. Every year, we would

take a trip to McAdenville to drive through the

neighborhood and admire the decorations. I crawled into

the back of the station wagon so that I could look out the

bigger window. The flashing snowmen and the twinkling

snowflakes lit up in my eyes and it lifted my spirits. I was

by myself in the back, just as content as I wanted to be. I

pretended that we were the perfect family again that always

had these kinds of outings. I pretended that Dad took me

out the car to walk around and see the lights up close. I

oohed and ahhed at the beautiful decor on the houses. Then I imagined that one of those houses was ours, big and beautiful and that we lived in that colorful neighborhood. I snapped back to reality at the sound of Shirl's voice screaming above Nat King Cole's Christmas Song. "You make me sick!" Shirl screamed. I jumped and my heart thudded as I turned around to see what the commotion was. Dad had moved to sit in the back beside Charity and Brian and Thomas. Apparently, this upset Shirl. Dad nodded to the music as if we were all having a pleasant time. She continued to scream and cuss the entire drive while Dad just sat there and smiled. He swayed to the music like a child and pointed out the window at the lights. I pitied him as he tried to make light conversation with us in hopes to tune out Shirl's rant. Her lipstick was now smudged and her face was no longer gentle as I had seen it earlier. Dad's eyes were tired and there was something so robotic about the way that he smiled. My heart longed to just hug him and not hate him anymore for the things he allowed. His beautiful skin was illuminated by all the lights and I noticed all the handsome features in his face that I blocked out so long before. I turned back around to face the back window, holding my breath to keep from crying. The sounds of Nat King Cole drowned out the sadness and despair felt so heavily in the car.

"And although it's been said, many times and many ways, Merry Christmas

to you."

School continued to be my favorite place. It was the only place that I could find peace and happiness. I transitioned from 3rd to 4th grade and the hardest part was no longer having Ms. Byrd as my teacher. She was the only one who understood me the most. I would only see her from time to time outside during recess or when my class would go to lunch. When I was granted a few moments with her, it was the highlight of my day. My new teacher, Mrs. Tindall, was nothing like Ms. Byrd. She always found a way to belittle my achievements. Whenever I would answer a question correctly or suggest a better way to do something, Mrs. Tindall would ask the class if they thought it was correct. She never applauded me when I solved a problem like she did my peers, and she never complimented me on my work after scoring 100% for most of my assignments. I had a feeling that Mrs. Tindall had spoken with Shirl and she believed that I was a troublemaker and as Shirl would say, "an attention whore." Mrs. Tindall rarely paid me any attention at all. Months had gone by and we received our progress reports to take home. According to my grades, I was the top student in my class. I couldn't wait to get home to tell Shirl and Dad. "We got our progress reports today!"

I said in a hurried voice as I ran through the open screen

door. Shirl was watching her stories in the living room so I

nervously extended my arm with my report to her. She

snatched it out of my hand, unenthused. I watched with

excitement as she opened it. She looked up at me, her face

looked like she had been sleeping all day. Lines were

etched across her forehead and her breath reeked like

alcohol. I could smell it from the distance I stood from her.

"What is this bullshit?" She shouted as she sat upright.

"You think you're all that little girl, don't you? You think

you're cute for getting good grades huh? Well you're not!"

She shouted as she stood from her seat on the couch. "And

no one is gonna give you any attention." She ripped the

report to shreds right in front of me, then stomped towards

the kitchen. I quickly bent down to pick up all the pieces

then I dumped them in the trashcan in the hallway. I flung

my book bag across my room so that it hit the wall and I

kicked and punched in the air with all the energy I had. I was boiling with anger, it's all that I could do to keep from yelling. I walked over to the window in the middle of our bunkbeds and put my head against it. I looked outside at some of my friends playing on the jungle gym and chasing each other around the grassy area. My body tinged with jealousy and rage. As I continued to watch them, I wondered why they got to play and how their parents rewarded them for their grades. It wasn't fair that I had to be inside when I made all "A's and it wasn't fair that every day, I had so much housework to do while Shirl sat and watched me do it. Then she would tell Dad how she cleaned the house spotless for him. I hated her with all my heart. She was a liar and a manipulator and it didn't matter where I went, she had a part in making my life completely miserable. I looked at all the smiling faces outside and my mind drifted from Shirl to reminiscing about all the fun and happiness we used to have. I thought about all the Saturdays that were filled with trips and fun adventures at the park with Dad. The happy thoughts lit my face up into a grin and I allowed those happy feelings to stay as long as they could. I was hurting inside and I was tired of Shirl's games and no longer feeling loved by Dad. I had gotten to the point that my body wouldn't allow me to cry anymore. I wasn't a baby and Charity always told me not to let Shirl see me cry. No matter how much Shirl continued to hurt me, I wouldn't let her get the best of me.

School slowly started to change for me, and it started to lose the spark that it once had. School no longer served as a safe haven for me but another place that caused me pain. My classmates took turns at calling me "Miss Know It All", because I knew more things than they did. Mrs. Tindall never stopped their taunts at my repeat outfits that I wore consecutively for weeks. She would simply glare at me just in case I decided to lash back. Whenever I would get in trouble at home, Shirl would make me wear the same outfit for the entire week so that I would be embarrassed by friends. My friends eventually stopped talking to me then stopped sitting with me at lunch. I stopped raising my hand whenever a question was asked, even though no one knew the answer in class. I was tired of being ridiculed for just wanting to be included and all I wanted to do was disappear. I would constantly hear Shirl in my head throughout the day saying, "Shut up, don't say anything." But it didn't matter how quiet I became, she never treated me any better. The beatings at home had gotten so severe that I was too weak at school to even fully participate. Some days I would sit out from recess because my legs and arms were too swollen from welts. Dad emphasized how we should tell our counselors that everything was fine at home and that we weren't being abused. I could no longer count on him for protection so I gradually did my best to disappear. I learned to talk low, make myself small, invisible almost to avoid any more problems than what I was faced with. I ended my 4th grade year sitting at a table with one bag of candy from a classmate whose Mom got every student a gift. All my other classmates had backpacks full of gifts and party bags from friends who would miss them for the summer. No one, not even Mrs. Tindall said anything to me as we ended our last day. I walked out the classroom towards the bus parking lot and never looked back.

10: "Answer me."

I've always lived in a fantasy world, where my reality was a place I constantly tried to escape from. When I played with my dolls, I always made sure they were perfect. I would comb the mommy Barbie's hair so that it looked nice and her clothes were always neat and pretty. "What do you want for dinner tonight sweetie?" I would say to the little doll as I pretended to be the mommy Barbie. "I want pizza and chicken!" I squealed, acting as the baby doll. I made sure that the mommy Barbie was always sweet and helpful to the babies and that she was happy to have them around. I found myself playing house with my dolls so often that I could tell if anyone had touched them. Before getting in bed, I placed the mommy doll in the right corner of my room and used a sock of mine to create a blanket for the baby dolls to lie down on. Everyone was ready for bed, so I turned the light off and drifted off to sleep. I woke up the next morning to the sound of a vacuum cleaner running in the hallway. I jumped up in shock, not sure of who was running it but I knew for sure it wasn't Shirl. I cracked the bedroom door just enough to peek through and saw the tall build of Dad's back facing me. I smiled in relief, glad that Charity and Brian weren't doing work without me. I would have felt guilty. I opened the bedroom door just as Dad shut the vacuum cleaner off. "Good Morning Dad." I said cheerfully. He turned around and nodded as he mumbled good morning. "What are you doing cleaning?" I asked. "It's filthy in here; this place needs to be cleaned!" He fussed. I immediately walked to the kitchen to grab the broom to start helping him. I looked around for Shirl but I didn't see her anywhere. I peeked back in the bedroom just once more before beginning to sweep and noticed that Charity had snuck back in the room and was playing with my mommy Barbie. I looked over to the corner and instantly noticed that the baby dolls were not on the sock anymore. I stomped into the room. "Where are the other dolls?" I asked Charity. "I don't know where they are?" she stammered. I saw a slight smirk appear across her face. "Yes, you do!" I shouted. "Where are my dolls? Give them to me!" I was furious that she found humor in moving the things that were important to me. I stood in front of her now, breathing fast with my face scrunched up. "I have no idea where they could be." she teased. My heart felt like it would beat out of my chest, I shook in trepidation and swiped my hand down to snatch my Barbie away from her. "Give me my dolls! I shrieked at the top of my lungs. "Oh my gosh, stop yelling at me!" Charity snapped as she stood up. At that moment Dad appeared in the doorway looking infuriated. "Where are the dolls?" He shouted. Charity quickly grabbed them out from her hiding place beside our bed. Dad stood there with his hands out as Charity reached them to him. He took the three dolls in his hand and immediately slammed them into the trash can right outside our room. My heart dropped and I shook my head in disbelief. "Now, stop all that yelling and get in here to help clean up." He said. I stood there as tears rolled down my cheeks. Not my dolls, I thought. I was devastated and couldn't bring myself to move my feet. Dad saw me staring at the trashcan and instantly grabbed the trash bag out and tied the handles in a knot. He turned around and marched out the front door. I sobbed as I heard the front door slam. I knew that my dolls were completely gone now and it was all Charity's fault. I felt like the entire world was against me. I jumped out of my daze as Shirl appeared out of her bedroom. She revealed a sinister grin and said, "Oh Well, you don't need to be playing with dolls anyway, aren't' you in middle school?" I stood there in silence, looking down at the floor. I didn't take the risk of looking her in the face while the flaming hatred I had for her showed on my face.

"Answer me!" Shirl shouted. I jumped again. "Yes ma'am, I am in middle school." "And you don't want to play with dolls." She said. I fidgeted as she waited for me to repeat her. "And I... I... do... do... don't wa... wa... wa... want to pa... pa... play with dolls." I stuttered.

"Good." She smiled and retreated to her room, slamming the door.

Middle school started for me with the transition to a new school but also a new home. We moved in with Grandma about a week before school started as Dad decided to finally leave Shirl. I thought that maybe he finally came to his senses about the abuse but it turns out, he had simply reached his wits end with the arguments and constant nagging that came with their relationship. In the beginning, a lot of their fights were about how Dad used to take up for us. He would always say to her, "You're too hard on them, you don't have to yell at them." And Shirl would always retort in a higher yell that ended in him cowering and allowing her to yell as much as she wants at us. The arguments progressed to being about the lack of time that Dad was home. She constantly accused Dad of cheating and never coming home when he was supposed to be. Those would always end in Dad leaving out the house and one of us getting beat on because of it. After a while, the arguments escalated to complaining about what our newborn sister needed and how that was more important than getting things for us. Dad brushed the whole moving thing over with us by saying, "She wasn't the right Mom for you guys." I chuckled to myself and mouthed the word Duh when he wasn't looking. I did my best not to analyze his statement or the nonchalance in his tone. It was safer for my emotions to pretend he never said anything about it at all. Being at Grandma's was a complete relief for me. Shirl had caused me to have regular panic attacks and my skin flared up so badly from eczema, that my right hand looked completely deformed. As the weeks went by, I was plagued with frequent nightmares of Dad deciding to go back to Shirl but Grandma reassured me that she was no longer a part of our family. It was an awkward time for me and my feelings towards the adults in my life but nevertheless, I was thrilled to be back playing outside and rolling down the hill with Charity in our skates. My favorite thing to do was to be outside and playing with Charity and Brian. I honestly didn't miss playing with Thomas, but I did wonder if he would miss us now that we moved away. I wondered if Shirl would treat him like she did us. I shook my head, knowing that wouldn't happen and I hoped that I would never have to see her again.

I was really excited to start the year at a new school and I had a new outfit to wear for the first day, thanks to Aunt Vivian!

Aunt Vivian surprised us by taking Brian, Charity and I to go school shopping. It had been a long time since we went shopping for new clothes. Dad usually got our clothes from churches or let us pick a few things out at the thrift stores but he hadn't taken us in a while. Once I picked out my new outfit, I couldn't stop looking at it. I was nervous to hand it to the checkout lady, unsure if Aunt Vivian would change her mind at the last minute. Shirl would always get us excited about things and then change her mind. It was one of her mind games she played. I learned to stop getting excited and just wait until things really happened. As we stood in the checkout line, I looked at Charity and Brian and hugged them, feeling like we had finally been saved. It felt that way because everyone started to take more time to do things with us. I hung my outfit up in the closet as soon as we got back to Grandma's and I would go in and check on it, every so often to make sure it was still there.

Charity and I became used to Aunt Vivian coming by Grandma's house on the weekends. She painted our nails and toes and let us look at all the magazines with models and beautiful ladies in it. She would wash and style our hair and even let me pick my favorite style from her hair book. My favorite thing was for her to put beads on my braids so that I could shake them every time I walked. Brian was always outside helping Grandad with his building projects or yard work. Our cousin Stone would come by and play basketball outside and sometimes he would bring us snacks from the neighborhood candy lady. He watched us after school when Grandma and Grandad weren't home. On some Saturdays, we would pack our things and go to Aunt Vivian's house where Stone lived and spend time with him there. She let us watch her cook and make all kinds of cakes and pies. We were her little taste testers and we loved filling our tummies with her delicious treats. "Aunt Viv, I'm really happy to be living with Grandma and being able to spend time with you." I said cheerfully. She smiled and said, "I'm glad y'all are here too."

11: "I am trying to help you."

My first week of school came and went just as fast as the weeks and months rolled by that followed. I was doing very well in my classes until Dad told us we had to move. Our move was so abrupt, I didn't have a chance to say goodbye to my friends or my teachers. Just as I was starting to feel safe and happy again, we moved to a hotel that was located not too far from Grandma's house. I was devastated to be leaving Grandma's and not being able to see Aunt Viv. "Were we too loud?" I asked grandma. "No, she replied. "Your Dad needs to take care of y'all, it cost an arm and a leg to take care of children and he can't ever just leave a couple dollars." She spat. I looked down at the ground. "Sorry, that we cost a lot, grandma. When I'm old enough, I'm gonna get a job and pay you back." I said softly.

The hotel we moved to was called Intown Suites and it was known to be an extended stay hotel for mostly people who were on the streets. You saw a little bit of everyone there, from drug dealers to prostitutes, homeless men and women, to high school dropouts that didn't want to live at home any longer. Dad told us to never open the door for anyone and go straight home after we got off the bus.

The most difficult part of the move for me was the task of starting all over at a new school. My first day at Smith Middle School was absolutely horrific, and it clearly set the tone for how the remainder of my year would be. I stepped on to the bus my first morning, eager to make new friends and there was no one that would allow me to sit down. As soft spoken as I was, I was terrified to ask if I could sit. I peered at the countless girls with their feet up against the seat barring my entrance, and I already knew what the answer would be. "Ughh, you ugly!" A boy shouted from the back of the bus. The entire bus erupted in laughter. The girls were slapping their knees and howling at his statement. I looked back at the bus driver as she prepared to take off. She gave me a look that said, "You're on your own kiddo." I gripped the seat in front of me to keep my balance as I stood. I made sure not to wobble too much or accidentally brush against the girl that was seated beside where I stood. She watched me the entire way to school, as if she was studying her prey. The kids on my bus were tough; I could just tell by the way they pronounced their words and all the cursing that came out their mouths. I realized quickly that the only way to survive was to be just like them. One day, as everyone started in on their daily jokes about how poor we were, living in a hotel, Charity lashed back at them, screaming, "Shut the hell up!" The entire bus froze and I believe I saw the bus driver raise her eyebrows. Everyone looked at Charity, and then looked at me, then back at her and there was silence for the rest of the bus ride. I couldn't have been any prouder! After that day, people started to treat us differently, and I knew it was because Charity proved that she wasn't going to take the bullying anymore. I was so appreciative that she had the guts to stand up to them and I prayed that I would find that backbone as well before she left to go to high school. The next year rolled around and Charity was off to a new school, which left me all alone. I was completely terrified because I knew she was the only reason no one messed with me. As the new year began, like clockwork, so did the bullying. There was a new set of kids that rode the bus this year, but they caught on quickly and joined in with the others. Each day it was something new, whether it was about my hair not being permed, the outfits that I wore consecutively or again how poor I was, no stone was left unturned. It was obvious that we didn't have any money. Dad was working countless hours but it didn't amount to much so we rarely got anything new. Dad didn't have much time to take us over to Grandma's so we didn't get to see them much. And because he worked so much, we rarely got to see him either. We were grateful for the times that Aunt Viv would pop up and bring us hot meals to eat and some of her delicious pie or cake that she baked. She would sit with us for a little while before we went to sleep and we would talk about school and everything under the sun. I found myself craving her food at school and dreaming about it when I went to sleep. There was a Wendy's and McDonalds right near the hotel, so Dad would leave us money to get dinner every night. It was a dream being able to eat mcflurries and fries every day but after a while I started to get sick of it.

"I don't want McDonalds tonight!" I yelled as Charity forced me to choose something on the menu one night. "Well you have to eat dinner Vivi, so pick something now!" Charity yelled back. "I'm not getting anything", I said softly, then went to sit down. Charity ordered food for me anyway and snatched the bag off the counter as it came up. "Let's go!" She growled at me. As we were walking out of the door, a lady from my school saw us and said hello." Hi, Mrs. Baker." I chimed sweetly." Hi Vivian." She replied. "Do you two have a ride?" She asked as she saw us beginning to walk. Before I could answer, Charity spoke up, "Yes we do." She said shortly. I looked down at the ground. "Ok, well I just wanted to make sure, because it's so dark out here." Mrs. Baker replied. "Yeah, we're good, thank you", Charity said with an attitude. "C'mon, Vivi." she demanded and started marching towards the hotel. I scurried behind her. "Why did you lie?" I asked Charity timidly. Charity quickly glared at me, then rolled her eyes. As we reached our building, a car pulled up beside us; it was Mrs. Baker. "Vivian!" She called. "Oh No!" I thought but before I could respond, Charity exclaimed, "Look lady this is our building, we're fine!"

"I understand that, "I'm just concerned that two, young girls are out at 9:00 at night walking by yourself. Anything can happen to you! Mrs. Baker retorted fiercely

"Are your parents upstairs?"

"Yes." Charity lied.

"Ok. well please be careful, and Vivian, I'll see you at school tomorrow." she ended.

"Ok", I said shamefully, then headed up the stairs behind Charity.

The next day I was called out of class and ushered to a room where the principal and yet another social worker sat, prepared to investigate our living arrangements.

I never believed that I was ugly, but after hearing it every day from students at school, my thoughts began to change.

Charity styled my hair and she did her best to tame my coarse mane but it was never as pretty as when Aunt Viv did it. My hair still stuck up in places and because it was so thick, I could rarely just put it into a ponytail. My big hair was usually all over the place. I didn't have the most stylish glasses but instead, the big plastic kind that were free each year with Medicaid. Somehow the kids all knew where my clothes, shoes and glasses came from and they made sure that everyone else knew as well. I always thought I looked decent when I looked in the mirror before leaving for school, but was convinced otherwise by the end of the day. The taunts became more and more outrageous each day. One morning, a quiet girl in the middle row of the bus, stood up as I approached her seat and said: "Don't even think about trying to sit with me, bleeding everywhere!" Everyone screamed in laughter. I had recently gotten my period and people knew because I had bled through my pants and had to keep my sweater wrapped around me all day. I was so ashamed. I was trying to understand everything that was going on with my body at the time and didn't have anyone to give me an explanation. Charity would tell me to make sure that I was going to the bathroom often so that I don't bleed out onto my pants. I didn't know how long it was supposed to last; I didn't know why my stomach hurt so bad; I was clueless. I stood there with my mouth open, in disbelief that this girl would say that. I wanted to sink into the floor and disappear but I couldn't. I had to go to class and deal with more hurtful slander from girls that looked just like me. Some of the same girls that picked on me, wore the same glasses I did and their hair was everywhere too. The bullying was relentless up until the bell rang that signaled the end of the day. I rushed out to the bus parking lot and got on bus #542 to head home. I stood as always near the front, looking at the sorry excuse for an adult, bus driver who smiled at the hateful kids that made my life hell. They brushed past me, intentionally nudging me enough to make me fall over into the occupied seats alongside me. "Ughh, get off me period girl!" A boy taunted. I gathered myself as the bus took off down the road. I counted down the time until my stop, just doing my best to focus on staying calm and breathing. My hands shook profusely and I burst into tears. I couldn't hold it in any longer. My breathing became frantic and I gasped as the sound of screams and laughter filled the air. "You're ugly, you're stupid, you're poor, you're lame, your hair is ugly, you need new clothes." Everyone took a turn at saying something that whirled in my head and played over and over again like a broken record. My vision was distorted from the tears that filled my eyes. I was hunched over when someone pushed my book bag. "We're at your stop!" the bus driver said. I steadied myself as I stumbled down the aisle to get off, doing my best to focus. Someone

pushed my book bag again, hard enough for me to stumble

forward. "Get your poor ass off of here." Someone shouted.

At that moment, as broken as I was, the adrenaline inside

me erupted and I snapped. I turned around and immediately

started throwing punches. I jumped on top of the boy who

was located right behind me. He was typically the

ringleader of all the bullying I endured. He put his arms up

to shield himself, but I kept punching. I refused to stop and

my body encouraged me to keep going; I had so much

energy. All I could think about was hurting him as much as

I was hurting. I was screaming and kicking and all of a

sudden, someone lifted me up and dragged me to the door

and down the steps. To my disbelief, it was the bus driver.

It was the first time I had ever seen her interfere with

anything. I stood still on the concrete in front of Intown

suites, breathing heavily. I watched the bus driver stomp

back up the steps. Fury ran through my entire being. She screamed at me, wagging her finger, "You know you gon' get suspended for this!" I laughed out loud at the suspension as a threat; it didn't scare me. I felt like I could do anything at that moment and it was the first time I smiled in a while. The bus sped off with shocked faces glaring out the window at me.

 The next day, Dad called a cab for me to take to school. Upon arrival to my classroom, I was called to the office. Just hearing my name announced on the intercom gave me chills. I slowly got up from my seat with a grin on my face as everyone eyed me. The bus fight had spread like wildfire throughout the school so everyone knew why I was being called. I entered the principal's office to see Jay, (the boy who I beat up) seated on the sofa. I sat beside him and looked up at a screen positioned beside the principal's desk.

A video started to play and I immediately knew it was the recording from the bus. All I saw was a girl swing around and start punching a boy behind her. "Whoa!" I said to myself. I was impressed by how strong I looked. There was so much commotion, you could barely hear anything. I saw the bus driver get up from her seat and break her way through the crowd that surrounded the fight. She lifted me up and then headed towards the door. The video cut off and the screen went black. I sat there trying to fix my face into a concerned and ashamed look. It was difficult because inside I was beaming with so much pride. I finally stood up for myself and I didn't need anyone to help me.

"What's your mother's name?" The principal asked. I hesitated to answer as the question made me nervous and caught me off guard. "Gwen Jones," I answered. It had taken me a minute to answer because I hadn't spoken her name in so long. The absence of my mom was something I rarely thought about because I didn't want to cause any more hurt for myself. Strangely enough, I entertained the idea that she would be proud of me for fighting. I wondered what she would say to me.

"Vivian!" The principal shouted, shaking me from my daydreaming thoughts.

"Yes", I answered, shifting in my seat.

"We tried getting in contact with her but the number was disconnected. Your father, David Jones, he hasn't responded to our calls, does he know about this incident?" The principal said it as if I was always in trouble.

"Of course, he knows, I wasn't able to ride the bus this morning." I retorted. The secretary in the office looked taken aback from my response. She shook her head and crossed her arms. "Well, you will be suspended from bus

542 for the rest of the week. You'll begin riding again on Monday. Are we clear?" the Principal said. I nodded. "You're dismissed." He ended. I got up and walked out the door with the least bit of regret. I didn't care and neither did Dad. Every time I would come home crying, he would look at me and tell me to stop. "Those kids that are talking about you are gonna be flipping burgers at McDonald's and you won't be." He would say. In his mind, that was reassuring enough, but it did nothing for me. I would just nod and wipe my tears.

My claim to fame was short lived and the school year ended as it began. This was the first time that I actually looked forward to summer break. I was completely exhausted from the school year. I remember sitting in an empty classroom on the final day, waiting for my social worker to tell me I could leave. She made a huge effort to see me before summer began and allow me space to talk about my feelings. I was failing all my courses except Creative Writing, and I refused to speak or participate in any activity. A lot of my teachers believed that I had a speech problem but were reassured by Ms. Peller, my Creative Writing teacher, that I simply chose not to speak. Ms. Peller hugged me before I left to see my social worker. She made sure to tell me that she looked forward to reading more of my writing upon return. "Thank you, Ms. Peller", I said softly. She was the only teacher that I spoke to. I was going to miss her encouraging words and praise for my daily journal entries. The most exciting thing about summer was having the chance to write more poetry and stories. Poetry was the one thing that gave me peace of mind. I would write while tears were falling from my eyes, when I was bubbling with anger or when I felt lonely. As soon as I put my pen down, a weight would lift from my shoulders.

Writing poetry was such an escape for me and it gave me a chance to explore my creative ideas. I was excited to see the look on Ms. Peller's face when I returned from summer break, with a journal completely filled with writing. She leaned back from our embrace and examined my face. "Vivian, sometimes when we can't control what's going on around us, we can always control how we respond to it, and we will never be powerless because of that." She said strongly. I nodded and smiled at her. "Have a good Summer." She said as I turned and headed down the hallway.

I headed towards the room that my social worker told me she would be located. She was so enthused about talking with me before the break but I didn't share her sentiments. She was aggravating to me. I dreaded talking to her because she always asked me the same questions. I had lost hope in what any social worker could do because they never helped, they only made things worse.

As I entered the empty classroom, she smiled brightly and said, "Welcome Vivian, happy last day of the school year!" I gave her a half smile back as I slowly pulled out a chair. "I have to run and make a copy and I'll be right back!" She said quickly and jetted out the door. I stared blankly at the white walls in the empty classroom, listening to the clicks of the clock marking each second. "Final call for bus riders, final call." Said a voice through the intercom speaker. I could faintly hear the buses beginning to leave the parking lot. My social worker skipped back through the door and slid two pieces of paper towards me. She grabbed her seat in front of me and adjusted herself. "Can we go over this one more time please?" She asked hesitantly. I sighed loudly in annoyance. "Please look at the picture Vivian," she directed. I looked at the naked picture of a woman with labeled body parts. "Has anyone ever touched you here?" She asked as she pointed to the breasts on the picture. I shook my head. "What about here or here?" She continued "No!" I shouted. "No one touches me, what does this have to do with anything?" I shouted. Her eyes widened in shock then she slammed her hand down on the desk. "I am trying to help you!" She gritted. "You are so difficult with your attitude and lack of desire to cooperate! Just forget it!" She waved her hand in the air and began gathering her papers furiously. I could tell that I upset her, but I didn't care. "Your attitude will get you nowhere in life." She snapped. "So, consider these meetings dismissed from now on, there's no help for you." She mumbled, then stomped out the door leaving me there, without a ride home.

12: "We don't know."

I was developing as a young woman and I was fascinated by all the changes that were taking place in my body. During this time, I also started to notice how my temperament changed. I remembered always being the soft spoken and gentle child, but I had become aggressive and easily upset. After the heated blowup with my social worker, I started to think that maybe she was right, maybe there was no help for me. I was turning into a mean person, just like Shirl and I didn't know how to stop it. I had mastered faking how I felt as a young girl, but I could no longer hide the expressions on my face. We moved back to Grandma's over the summer, which meant another school change. Dad continued to work long hours so our time with him had no improvement. Whenever he came by the house, our visits were very short-lived; he always had somewhere else he needed to be. We spent the majority of our time with Aunt Viv and Grandma. I also noticed little things about my family that I hadn't seen before. Whenever we would go somewhere, I was always reminded to make sure my hair was neat and laid down. At the time, Charity was still doing my hair but because I had so much of it, styling was a big ordeal. Charity would become frustrated and yell at me saying, "You need to do it yourself!" I had no idea where to start, so it was usually brushed back into a poofy, lopsided ponytail. I was on my own with styling and was doing a terrible job at it. I tried to figure out how to style myself so that I could look more trendy. Appearance was everything to my family. I noticed that if we didn't look decent, we either stayed at home while they went somewhere or it was an all-day event to get our clothes and hair together for an outing. I never wanted to embarrass them, we just didn't have much. A lot of our clothes were worn down and tattered. Grandma used to fuss about why

Dad even allowed us to put those things on. She would go out and buy a couple outfits for each of us and tell us how much money it cost her to get us some "nice-looking clothes." I constantly felt bad because Grandma would make sure to tell us how much the dinner cost each time we ate, how much the water bill was whenever we would take baths and how much more money she would have if Dad took care of us. I never understood why Dad never had time to see us. I thought about my mom, Gwen, and why she wasn't there to help take care of us either. Nothing made sense to me so that summer, I decided to write letters to people that I needed answers from. Ms. Peller emphasized the need to use different forms of writing to express yourself. I loved short stories and poetry but writing letters seemed perfect for everything I wanted to say. She slipped a notebook into my bag before I left for the summer and wrote a note inside that said, "This journal is for you to write whatever you feel."

The first letter I wrote was addressed to Dad.

 Dear Dad,

Why are you never here with us and why do you not take care of us? Grandma told us that you never give her any money to help with things that we need and that's not fair to her. She's our grandmother but not our Mom. I want to know what happened with Mom. Where is she and why isn't she here to take care of us?

Sincerely,

 Vivian

I let Charity read over my letter to see what she thought.

"That is bad, Vivi, why would you write that?" She barked.

"Because it's true, and because I want to know the answers," I said.

"No. That's being disrespectful. You shouldn't say that to your Dad," Charity retorted. Charity talked about Dad like he was an angel and it blew my mind how she continued to have hope in him. I admired her for it, but sometimes I wanted her to snap out of it. Something inside me just told me to keep the letter to Dad and write one to Gwen as well. I wrote a letter to her with the most heartfelt things I wanted to say. I didn't remind her of her absence, or the pain it had caused but I simply said, "I hope you're doing ok and I just want you to be happy." That's what I truly wanted for her. I heard so many stories of how Dad decided to leave her when we were younger. I heard that she wasn't happy with the life of a military wife living on a base, so she wanted to find a way to leave. I also heard that she got strung out on drugs and was no longer able to care for us so Dad decided to leave. That was Grandma's version. What I never heard was her side of the story or a story that didn't place one person at blame. Despite how many times I was told that Gwen was a horrible person, I couldn't bring myself to hate her. No one could be worse than Shirl. She is the one person I truly hated.

 I asked Grandma for Gwen's address and a stamp and she gladly gave it to me. I sent my letter off the next day. Weeks went by, and it dawned on me that I hadn't gotten anything back in the mail. I questioned if I had written the address correctly or if my mail had been misplaced. But I knew it hadn't; I knew she didn't write back. Maybe she didn't know how to reach out like I did or she needed help talking about things. I also thought that my letter could have made her feel embarrassed and she was ashamed that she wasn't there for me when I needed her. I played with these ideas in my head until they made me feel better and until the tears stopped falling on my lap.

Summer was a complete bore so whenever Charity, Brian and I got a chance to get outside, we jumped at it. We went for a walk around the neighborhood one early Saturday morning and ventured to the candy lady to get some treats. "Ding,ding", the bell jingled as we opened the screen door to go inside the candy lady's house. The smell of chocolate and sweet cake filled the air and an instant smile was painted on my face. I marvelled at all the colorful packages of candy and chips, trying to decide how to just pick one. I had a total of $2.00 in assorted coins jingling in my pocket but couldn't decide what would be worthy. I scanned the variety of chips laid out on a table in a corner then moved over to another table full of mini chocolates and gummies. "What's your favorite kind sweetheart?" A raspy voice spoke out. I jumped, looking up to see a slender woman with a scarf tied around her hair. "I love the laffy taffys." I said softly. "20 cents each and same thing for the mini snickers, so get as many as you want." She said hurriedly. I stood there, waiting for her rushed speech to process in my brain. She talked very fast. "You here to see your mother young man?" She asked Brian. He was just as confused as Charity and I, as he looked around, then replied: "No, we just wanted to get some candy." She peered at the three of us and the bewildered looks on our faces, then turned around and left the room. We looked at each other and I instantly became tense. There was something weird about her. Charity nodded towards the screen door and we followed behind her, dropping our gathered snacks on the table on our right. "Brian." A soft voice, very different from the candy lady's raspy speech, called out. Charity's hand was on the door handle and she froze in midstep. I heard Brian breathe heavily and slowly slide his shoes around to face the woman speaking. I slowly turned my body to face her as well. "You look so much like your Dad." She beamed. I gasped as she came around the counter and approached us. The first thing that I noticed was her eyes, they were small and beautifully slanted like Charity's. Her cheekbones were high and regal and her complexion was the exact caramel tone as Charity's as well. There was a long silence, then she spoke. "Hi baby," she said as she looked at me. I knew who she was. Despite her dark hair standing up all over her head and the missing teeth in her mouth, I knew her name was Gwen. She was my Mom. She bent down to hug me and I stood motionless, unsure of what to do. I held my breath as she embraced me, trying to block out the foul smell of alcohol and smoke that lingered on her clothes. She rubbed her hand across my cheek and I stepped back, and grabbed ahold of Charity. "What's wrong?" She asked, slowly standing back up. "She doesn't know you." Charity snapped. "I'm your Mom, baby," she mouthed in my direction. "Let's go," Charity demanded. I didn't understand why Charity was upset. "Wait...please wait." Gwen begged. I held Charity and Brian's hand as she reached out to hug us again. "I love you guys so much, I want you to know that." I stared at her intensely. I couldn't turn away. Everything about her was like nothing I had seen before. She smiled a smile that seemed so familiar and I couldn't help but smile back. "Ya'll don't want your snacks?" The candy lady interrupted. She could tell from my expression that the answer was yes but I didn't reply after seeing the look on Charity's face. "Well, ya'll come back and see me ok." The candy lady said in record speed. We left out the door and started to make our way back to Grandma's.

"Why does she look like that?" I blurted out. "She's on drugs Vivi, can't you tell?" Charity snapped. "Well how

- 125 -

did you know that was our Mom?" I pressed. "Because I've

seen her before. Me and Brian have. We remember her

from when we were younger but you were just a baby. She

was the best Mom to us." Charity said sadly.

"So what happened to her?" I looked at both Charity and

Brian when I asked.

"We don't know Vivi." "We don't know."

We walked the rest of the way back in silence.

That night, after helping Charity wash the dishes from

dinner and listening to Grandma talk about how high the

light bill was, I sat down in the living room and pulled out

my journal. I flipped through the pages and noticed that

Ms. Peller had written a writing prompt on one of the last

pages. The prompt read: "What is love and what does it

look like?"

I quickly wrote on the next line, "Love is not being afraid

to have difficult conversations. Love looks like a mom

telling her story to her daughter so she doesn't feel

abandoned. Love is a dad saying sorry for not protecting

his daughter from a woman who could never fill the role of

a mom. Love is apologizing and love is also forgiving.

13: "I'm going to stay here."

"Hey guys, I found you another Mom!" Dad said eagerly.

We all looked up from the books we were reading, doing

our best to appear excited by the news. "I want you guys to

meet her, so let's go!" Dad said. We hopped in his station

wagon, Charity and Brian both piling in the back, and me,

taking the front seat. Dad happily sped down the road from

Grandma's house. I brought my book along to ease the

awkward silence that typically happened with Dad. As I sat

up front, I hoped that he didn't ask me any questions about

school, or how I felt about him; I wasn't a really good liar.

Thankfully, he clicked on his Phil Collins tape and

hummed along to it as he drove. I looked up from my book

periodically to see him still in a pleasant mood. He made a

right turn into a familiar place – Golden Corral. It was one

of our favorite places to eat and of course, it was where

Dad worked. "Dad, can we eat here?" Brian leaned up to

ask. "Yes, Beanhead, you guys can eat here." Dad laughed. Beanhead was his playful name for us. As soon as we walked in, all of Dad's coworkers greeted us as if we were celebrities. I smiled and followed a lady to a table where she had some plates set up for us. I laid my book down on the booth seat and made a beeline for the salad bar. I was excited to get as much fruit on my plate as possible and of course a bowl of ice cream with unlimited toppings! Charity was on my right, piling her plate with strawberries and honeydew. Brian was behind her making a salad. Once our plates were filled with colors, we headed back to our table. We saw Dad standing there with a tall, red-headed woman, laughing hysterically. We slid over on the booth seats and looked up at them. The lady was still laughing as she wiped one of her eyes. "She's laughing at this joke I just told." Dad began. It goes like this, "So a guy walks up and says, hey what's your name?" The other guy answers,

"My name is Jim; what's yours?" The other guy replies by saying, "People around here call me Blue Cheese."

"Well, why they call you that?" Jim replies.

"Cuz' I be Dressing!" said the guy.

Dad instantly let out an obnoxious snort and taps the table in laughter. The red-haired woman puts her arm on him as if she can't stand from laughing so hard. I chuckled slightly then looked over at Charity. She had a puzzled look on her face as she didn't understand the joke. "I'll explain it to you later", I whispered. Charity smiled and nodded along with everyone. I looked at the way the red-haired woman clung to Dad as she settled herself from her laughing fit. "This must be the new lady", I thought to myself. Dad turned to us just as I put some fruit in my mouth. "Guys I want to introduce you to Kim." He pointed to us and said, "These are my beanheads." She waved and said hello. We nodded back at her, unable to speak because we were all chewing.

"She's got to get back to work, but I just wanted you guys to meet her." Dad said nervously. He turned swiftly and followed her giddily, wherever she was going. We all looked at each other with shocked faces. We all waited to see who would speak first. I looked at Charity, then to Brian, holding back a grin as it crept up my face. Charity instantly spoke up, " Oh my gosh, she's white!" She exclaimed. I put my hand over my mouth and raised my eyebrows several times. We all laughed. "Is that going to be our new mom?" Charity leaned in to ask. Brian shook his head and said, "I hope not, I'm tired of new moms. "Yeah me too." Charity agreed. We sat there and enjoyed the rest of our meal.

Shortly after beginning my 7th grade year, Dad moved us into a 1-bedroom apartment with Kim. We saw her a few more times after our initial introduction but never got to know her. Grandma and Aunt Viv were upset with Dad because he was making us switch schools for the umpteenth time. Grandma insisted that we stay with her for the remainder of the school year so we didn't suffer from the transition. I was surprised at her lack of joy for us leaving. I always thought we were a hassle for her. Aunt Viv was angered by the constant instability that came with Dad, but he refused and demanded that they stay out of his business. It would be awhile before we saw them again.

"Have y'all done your homework?" Kim asked shyly. We were all sitting near the TV, in the living room area, watching Peter Pan. "Why?" Charity snapped from the couch. "Because your Dad said to make sure that y'all did it." Kim retorted. "Hmm, that's interesting", Charity said as she stood from the couch and approached Kim. "Last time I checked, Dad had a mouth of his own. He can ask me that himself. Charity stood perfectly still in front of Kim's frightened frame. I was turned completely around on the couch, watching Charity in awe. "Is that clear?" Charity pressed. Kim turned around dramatically and walked to her room, slamming the door loudly. "Humph!" Charity said as she turned around and winked at me. I giggled. I loved how fiery she was; she always spoke her mind. I always wished I could be as strong as her. "He doesn't need somebody else to speak to his children for him. Am I right?" Charity belted. She walked in a circle as if delivering a speech to a large crowd. "And he definitely doesn't need anyone telling his kids to clean up and do chores for somebody who isn't even their MOTHER!" She riled loud enough for Kim to hear. I pumped my fist in the air in solidarity with her. "That's right Charity, Brian said strongly. "We don't have to listen to her." "Nope!" I said shaking my head. We can do what we want!" I said smiling.

That night, we were awakened by Dad screaming at us, telling us to stand against the wall. He cut on the lamp in the living room area where we had our sleeping bags spread out on the floor. "Charity come over here." He demanded. Charity left my side and stood in front of Dad. I looked to my right to see Kim standing with her arms crossed in the doorway that separated the living area from her bedroom. "I heard you were being disrespectful to Kim today." Dad began. "I didn't disrespect her, I told her you can ask us what you need to and you can speak for yourself." Charity answered. "Well Kim said you disrespected her and had her blood pressure up so turn around", he said as he reached for his belt. He began to beat Charity in front of us until she dropped to the ground in pain, then called us one by one to receive the same fate. I stood shaking against the wall after being hit repeatedly by the belt. "From now on, you do exactly what she says, you call her Mom and you don't talk back", Dad yelled. "If I hear anything, I'll beat you like this again until you do things right. Am I Clear!" He shouted. Brian stood with tears running down his face and nodded. Charity looked down at the ground and refused to acknowledge him. And I stood there in shock and disappointment of the hero I once believed in. I looked over at Kim to see her smiling, then they both ventured back into their room shutting the door loudly.

That night I couldn't sleep. I stayed awake trembling in fear of Dad. His shouts echoed in my head and I was nervous that he would wake us up again to beat us. I wanted more than anything to be able to fly away like Peter Pan to Neverland. I wished that Charity, Brian and I could go to a place where no one would mistreat us. I prayed to God that night to help us and to change Dad back into who he used to be. I believed that God would help us. Grandma always said that God was the only one we could call on.

A few months had passed and Dad announced that Kim was pregnant. I was utterly confused because Dad would go over scriptures in the bible with us and he taught us that we should not have sex before marriage, yet they weren't married. He noticed the confused looks on our faces. "I know what I've taught you guys but I prayed and asked for forgiveness to God so everything is ok. Aren't you guys excited that you're gonna have a little brother?" Dad asked excitedly. "No." Charity said.

"You don't have to like it, but you will continue to respect Kim." Dad retorted. Tensions hadn't eased from the initial conflict Charity had with Kim. She hadn't spoken much to Dad since the incident and I could tell that her solid faith in Dad was slowly dwindling.

Charity stood there with a fierce look on her face then yelled out loudly, "Dad, I'm so sick of you listening to all these women and never listening to us! I'm ready to leave! I will live anywhere else but here!" She turned her back on him and walked back towards the kitchen table. "I'll live on the street if I have to, I just don't want to be here!" Charity shouted.

"Dad stomped into the living room, "Pack your stuff then Charity, since you want to be so smart." "I want to leave too." Brian chimed in. "Well you can go too, Dad muttered back, unphased. I looked at Brian, then over at Charity in horror. "If you don't want to follow directions, leave!" Dad shouted.
Everyone looked at me, waiting for me to speak. I was shaking from the idea of Charity and Brian leaving me. "What are you going to do?" Dad pressed. "I am go… go…

going to sta… stay here," I said in fear. He swiftly turned back around to face Charity. "Go on and get your stuff", he said to them. Charity and Brian started to pack their stuff. Dad's voice trailed off into the bedroom. He returned after a few minutes, speaking calmly. "Y'all can go and stay with your mom and let her take care of you." Charity looked up after stuffing her sleeping bag in her case. My heart broke as our eyes connected. "Noooo, don't go," I whispered.

"I have to Vivi, I can't take this anymore. I'm going to end up beating her ass if she tells you or me what to do again. I would probably hit her in her stomach, that's how mad I am. Forgive me Lord", she looked up and said.

"But am I going to see you again?" I cried to her. "Just come with us Vivi, you don't have to stay here."

"But I don't want to leave Dad, I will feel bad if I do." I stammered. I was so torn because I really wanted to leave with Charity and Brian but I didn't want to disappoint Dad.

I was crushed either way. A car outside honked and Dad went to open the door. There was a yellow cab parked in front of the apartment we stayed in. Charity and Brian struggled to carry their things out to the car. It was pouring down raining and Dad just stood there and watched. I went to stand at the door and my entire body wanted to give up and topple to the ground. My best friends were leaving me, with no given idea of when we would see each other again. My heart was hurting and I couldn't stand to watch the cab drive off so I turned around and headed for the bathroom. Before I did, I mouthed the words, "I love you" to Charity who was looking out the window. I stayed in the bathroom for a long time crying. Kim knocked on the door, in hopes of coaxing me out of the bathroom and me running into her arms to cry. Instead, I opened the door and headed straight to my sleeping bag. I covered my head and cried myself to sleep.

14: "You're being selfish."

Shortly after giving birth to their first child, Dad announced that Kim was pregnant again; this time with twins. We moved to a new place where the new babies would have their own room as I continued to share a room with my newborn brother. I started my first year of high school wishing that I left with Charity and Brian. They went to stay at Gwen's mom's house. My spirits were lifted every chance I got to talk to them on the phone. I wanted to know how it was living over there and what was different. Charity told me about how they both had their own room and they could do what they wanted. Gwen's mom took them shopping for school at Old Navy and they got brand new clothes and shoes! I couldn't believe it. I looked down at the tattered jeans I had on and wished that I could be there with them. It would be great to have new clothes but what I wanted more than anything was to be with them every day.

Things became tough for me, immediately after they left. All of the chores in the house became my responsibility and there was a certain time I had in order to get it all completed. After school, I would drop my backpack at the table in the living room and head straight for the bathroom. I wiped the counters down first and then scrubbed the toilet last. I swept and mopped and headed to the living room after I was finished. I pulled out the vacuum cleaner and began pushing it slowly around the floor. Kim would watch me from the couch as she clicked the volume button on the television so that her shows wouldn't be disrupted by my cleaning. I was always so busy with cleaning the house and helping out with my younger brother, that I had no time for socialization. I wanted to make friends badly and was even more interested in getting to know guys at my school but

Dad always said I didn't have time for a boyfriend and needed to focus on my studies. I always thought that he would eventually come around but he didn't. I just continued to stay busy with chores and babysitting throughout my semester.

It seemed as if the announcements would never end. After the twins were born, Kim told me that she was pregnant once again. Once my fourth brother was born, we moved to Raleigh, away from everyone that I knew and closer to Kim's family. Kim became pregnant once more with another boy and there was no announcement. Kim had a huge stomach and sat around all day, so it was hard to tell the difference. With each new child that came into the house, I was expected to do more and more for my siblings. It started with simply helping with bottles at night, changing diapers here and there, to continuous nights of Kim and Dad going out and me being left at home to babysit my brothers. I would be invited out with friends but would always have to decline due to Kim and Dad wanting to go out and not watch the boys. I loved my brothers deeply so the time we spent together wasn't in vain. I read them stories, acted out movies, cooked for them, cleaned their messes, tucked them in at night, woke them up for school, and held them when they were crying. They would always run in the middle of the night and get in my bed. I was their mother and they brought me happiness as children do, but life was miserable.

I remember the day I got my wisdom teeth pulled. I was in so much pain but I was more relieved to simply have a moment to not have to do anything. My cheeks were so swollen, I looked like a chipmunk on the way home from the dentist. I was ready to lay down once arriving home but instead, Kim immediately told me to wash the dishes.

Without any feeling in my mouth, drool slipped from my numb lips onto my t shirt. I put my hand in my mouth to push the gauze back as far as I could. It was difficult to control the bleeding and the medicine that I was given still had me extremely drowsy. I moved very slowly.

"Vivian, can you bring me a fork?" Kim yelled from her bedroom. I walked in the room to see her sitting Indian style on the bed with her food on her lap. "Oh my gosh, thank you so much, I know I'm being lazy. I just got into a good spot and didn't want to move." She said nonchalantly. I nodded, waiting for her to acknowledge the blood on my shirt. "If you're done with the dishes you can go back and lay down if you want." She said. I turned around and headed back into the kitchen to finish the dishes, dragging my feet down the hallway. Once I finished, I finally reached my bed completely exhausted and had no energy left to clean my bloody shirt. I covered my pillow with a towel just in case I would bleed out anymore then faded into a deep sleep quickly. I woke up hours later to feel a small body beside me sleeping. I smiled, realizing the feeling had returned to my mouth then slowly drifted back to sleep.

I barely graduated high school due to the instability of my home life. I was plagued with constant late nights of helping Dad and Kim with the boys and being involved in the chaos of their relationship. My grades suffered severely, but thankfully I graduated and was admitted into a local community college. I received my first cell phone as a graduation gift and I was so excited to finally have something of my own. I remember Dad telling me that he would check my phone to make sure I didn't get any guy's numbers on campus. I thought if he planned to check my phone, that defeated the purpose of him giving it to me so I didn't want it. I was tired of being controlled. I had gotten to the point that Charity had been when she stood up and said she wanted to leave. I wanted to live somewhere else because I was miserable. All my friends stopped inviting me out because I was never allowed to do anything. I had no life outside of the house. I felt like my life was on pause until Kim and Dad decided they were both ready to assume their responsibilities. But until then, I continued to do as I was told, praying that things would change.

One day our neighbor Robert had popped by to say hello. He and his wife would have me babysit their two children when they went out on dates. Their idea of me babysitting was having the kids already in bed so that I could relax and watch tv and have a meal to myself. They knew all the work that I did with my brothers and they wanted to find a way to help me. They would order a large pizza with wings, and soda. They would have their kids in bed and tell me to make myself at home. Not only would they make sure I wasn't working but they would send me back home with $50 in my pocket.

Robert rang the doorbell and I hurried to open the door. A roach scurried across the front door just missing his shoe. "How's everything going?" He asked me. "Everything is good," I smiled. I was doing my best to position myself in the door frame hoping to keep his attention away from a roach that was crawling on the floor behind me. The sympathy in his eyes was apparent. My living conditions were pitiful and it was obvious that I had no control over my circumstances. Robert asked if I would be available on an upcoming Saturday to babysit. I thanked him for stopping by and promised to get back with him when I knew if I was available. I closed the door feeling completely embarrassed. I looked down at the stained carpet and dirty baseboards.

My thoughts were interrupted by miscellaneous roars echoing from the hallway. My brothers were fighting again. I sighed, hoping Dad and Kim would get home soon. They called an hour earlier to tell us we would be going to the park that afternoon. I was excited about getting out of the house and doing something as a family. I got the boys washed up and ready in record time. We sat together, huddled on the couch, and anticipated their arrival.

2 pm came and went.

2:30 passed.

3:00 snailed by and then it was 4:00.

They didn't even call. We sat on that couch, gazing at the puke colored walls, watched the sun set and accepted that they weren't coming to get us. More false hope and daily disappointment. I closed the blinds and got right to my nightly "mom" duties. As we ate at the dinner table, I did my best to embrace the reality that Dad didn't care about any of us. The only thing that mattered was the woman in his life.

I always wanted the best for Dad. But I resented him for the way that he allowed Kim to treat me. I thought many times about why I stayed and didn't leave. There would be days where I would work tirelessly and just before laying down Kim would demand a venting session about the atrocious relationship they had. Kim would vent to me about Dad and how he wasn't faithful. She always talked about how black men always did women wrong, and how her mixed children were going to resent their father because of how he treats her. I remember nodding off as she talked about him looking at another woman when they were out earlier. She asked me what I thought about that, and I told her that I didn't care.

"I've been up since 7 am this morning, fixing the boys breakfast, while you slept in." I began. I took them outside and played with them for most of the day, came in to make all 5 of them lunch, cleaned the kitchen, did their laundry and started dinner as you and Dad prepared to leave and go out. I completed dinner, cleaned the kitchen, gave all your 5 boys a bath and put them in bed. I am exhausted and I want to go to sleep, so I don't care!" I shouted. She got up from her bed and slapped me across my face. "You are a disrespectful little bitch," she shouted back. I put my head down to the floor. The stench of alcohol lingered on her breath as she continued to shout at me. Dots of spit flew on my face as she continued to yell. I closed my eyes and wished so hard that I could disappear. I hated her. I hated Dad for never being there. My entire life, I was put off on someone else who never cared for me like a mother should. He was forever trying to find a replacement for Gwen, and a substitute for the love I deserved. He forgot that I still had him and that he could still sustain me with his love, but it never came. Kim continued to shout at me that night: "This is why your dad doesn't deal with you and tells me to deal with you." She would carry on by saying that I wasn't popular in school and didn't have friends because I talked too much. She told me countless times how much of an airhead I was and said that was the reason why I failed in my math classes. I didn't care, I just wanted to go to sleep. I was sick and tired of everyone and I hated my life.

As I stared at the floor and took in insult after insult, feeling like a complete slave to a master who was never satisfied; I told myself I wouldn't break down. All I wanted to do was sleep. If I could sleep, I could stand there forever and listen to her shout. But that night, that's all I wanted and she knew that. She decided to make me stand up against the wall instead of going to bed since I was being "disrespectful".

I woke up early, the next morning after a couple hours of rest to fix my brothers some breakfast. I splashed some cold water on my face and reached for a towel to dry. I looked in the mirror and I hated what I saw. I couldn't have stopped myself from breaking down even I wanted to. Tears began to pour out full blast and I sobbed into the towel to muffle my sadness. I felt like the only people that really loved me were my brothers.

As much time as I took to play with them and make up games and tell scary stories, they thought I was the best person in the world. It was the highlight of my day, being with them, nevertheless, it was tiring and I was overwhelmed. I remember looking into Kim's eyes the night before and knowing that I hated her. She was just like everyone else in my life, doing everything they could to use me. Dad allowed her to use me, told me to call her mom when she was nowhere close to treating me like a daughter. She never loved me and she definitely never loved him. There were times during these days that I questioned if Dad even cared about me. I wondered if I was just there to be their slave and because it was convenient for him to still have one of his children that was capable of helping out around the house. It seemed that the work that I did was the only thing that I was good for, so I questioned if he even loved me. He was rarely home and whenever he was; he barely looked at me; he barely came and said hello or made an effort to tell me that I was important. He never made me feel special or even acknowledged my existence. I asked myself: "Where is that guy that used to asked me about my day and call me his Vivi Dove?" I questioned his love every day but most importantly, I started to become numb and not think about love at all. I felt completely alone and no longer wanted to live.

After months went by of more ridicule from Kim, I no longer desired love from Dad and had completely blocked out my emotions towards everyone. Dad had walked past me several times after coming home to see me holding several books above my head in a corner. Kim had told him that I had been there for an hour because I did something airheaded. He walked past me as if I was invisible and headed towards the kitchen. My brothers would come up to

- 154 -

me laughing and poking my legs chanting, "Mommy said you're stupid, stupid Vivi, stupid Vivi." While I stood there, shaking from the weight of the books and pain in my arms, I realized that Dad would never put me first. I recognized the pattern of a woman always standing in the way of everything that I wanted from him. It hurt me tremendously, to the point that I contemplated the idea of taking my own life. I would fantasize about everyone crying at my funeral, declaring that they should have treated me better. I didn't want to exist anymore as the outcast that was only good for working and cleaning the house. I knew the best thing for me to do was disconnect in order to survive. I completely stopped caring because I knew that my downfall was loving with the belief that it would be reciprocated.

"Dad, Kim, I am leaving to go and stay with Aunt Vivian in Charlotte." I stood in the living room shaking as they both looked at me from the couch.

"Why do you want to go stay there?" Dad asked curiously. "I hope you realize that you are abandoning your family." He said. "And I hope you realize that you're leaving the boys and you're going to break their hearts."

I couldn't believe what I was hearing.

"You're being really selfish." Kim sneered.

I couldn't get another word out and instantly broke down crying. I felt so stuck. My brothers meant the world to me. If it wasn't for them, I would have taken my life long before then. I was worried that they would be treated the same way I was, if I decided to leave. I would miss waking them up every day, seeing them off to school and hugging them when they came home. The last thing I wanted to do was hurt my brothers but I knew that my life depended on leaving; I couldn't stay there any longer. They were too young to understand everything that was going on, but I knew how they felt and I was their mom. I was the one that cared for them and spent time with them. I just wanted to be free. I just wanted time to breathe and have a moment to myself to figure out who I was. It was hurtful to be told that I was selfish for leaving, but I made a promise that day that I would do whatever it took to ensure that my brothers knew they were loved. I believed that they would grow up and I would be able to explain to them why I left and why I wasn't there for them. It was one of the hardest things in my life to do but I knew I needed to do it.

I packed my bags and left for good.

15: "You just haven't had the experiences that others have..."

I never knew what freedom was or how it felt until I moved in with my Aunt Vivian. I had secured a job working at Golden Corral and was elated to be told each day that I was an exceptional team member. I couldn't believe that I had my own room, I could go and come as I pleased and didn't have to ask permission to hang with friends. I enjoyed spending time with my aunt and quickly grew closer to her as we shared more memories together. She was a part of so many firsts for me. She took time to teach me how to drive as Kim refused to allow me to take drivers ed while I was in school. Aunt Viv pushed to help me achieve independence and be able to do things for myself. After failing the driving test twice, I felt like everything that Kim and Shirl said about me was right. I couldn't shake the belief that I was stupid and that I wouldn't be successful at anything. But Aunt Viv told me not to be discouraged and did her best to remind me of how special she thought I was. "You just haven't had the experiences that others have and it is ok, you are going to do this!" She said. I went back the following week and I passed the driving test and finally received my license. It was such a huge moment for me because I finally proved to myself that I could accomplish something on my own. I was so proud of myself.

Aunt Viv also taught me how to style my hair and took me to the salon to have it done. It was a new feeling for me, finally being back with someone who cared and wanted the best for me. She was a mom to me like no one else had ever been.

One day I burst through the front door, completely excited because a guy asked me out. I didn't know what to do with myself! I remember his expression when I told him I needed to ask for permission. I sputtered the details to Aunt Viv, and asked if I would be able to go. She replied nonchalantly, "You don't have to ask me. Go enjoy yourself!"

I was so startled by her answer because I just knew that she would say no. I was so accustomed to being denied what I wanted that I still struggled with the feeling of anxiety. I was feeling that any minute, things might change and I would be in trouble. My mind was constantly preparing for defeat, but it never came.

My first date was everything I could have imagined it would be. It slowly developed into my very first relationship and I became completely consumed by it. I was 19 years old with the heart of a 14-year-old, very fragile and naive. I was so intrigued because I never experienced spending time with a guy, dating or falling in love. Needless to say, I fell hard for him. In my mind, I believed that he was my Prince Charming and he had come to rescue me from my castle. I planned out our life together like a crazed teenager, scribbling his name in my journals; fascinated by how being in love felt. Life began to speed up as I opened up my heart to him. The years swiftly passed and before I realized it, I was a mature woman. It had been four years since I left Dad and Kim in Raleigh, and it was four years of dating a man and experiencing life like I've never known! Everything was incredible for me. As sweet as the newness of love tasted, I realized that there is such thing as overindulging. My first relationship ended in heartache after discovering that I was being cheated on for the entirety of it. This realization broke me down and again reminded me of all the things I was told as a young girl. I was reminded of the taunts and yells from people I had blocked out of my mind; they all came back to the forefront. I did my best not to give energy to those things. I made up in my mind that my life would not be built on the constant disappointment from others, but by how I dealt with it. It took some time for me to heal and grow from that broken relationship but I was determined to be happy again.

My dream has always been to go college and pursue a degree. I decided to apply to my dream school; Winston Salem State University, and I was accepted. I previously enrolled in a few classes at the local community college but desired to transfer and experience college life. I believed that if I blocked the ideas of others about me, I could be successful. After receiving my acceptance letter, I posted it on my wall in my room and it kept me motivated for the weeks leading up to my departure. As I looked around my room at my packed belongings, it finally hit me that I was leaving home to truly be on my own. Aunt Viv and my cousin Stone drove me to Winston Salem and helped me move into my dorm. It didn't take us long to move things in because I didn't have much, but we did work up an appetite. We went to a nearby fish place and stuffed our faces! After hours of laughs and getting settled in, Aunt Viv said she had to get back on the road as it was getting late.

My eyes instantly began to water.

I was dreading this part.

I was nervous and didn't know the first thing I would do on my own and wasn't quite ready to face things alone. I also didn't realize how attached I had gotten to being around family again while living with her. It was a brand-new life for me and she was there for me like no one else had ever been. I didn't want her to leave but I knew she had to. I walked her down to the entrance of my dorm building and hugged her for as long as I could. I hugged Stone and they got back in the van and both waved goodbye. It was time for me to be brave.

I found my voice in college and discovered how different it was from middle and high school almost immediately. I think I was expecting everyone to look at me strangely and treat me like I didn't belong, but it was quite the contrary. I quickly made friends and started to embrace a more positive self-image of myself. I fell in love with the classes that I was taking and was excited to complete every assignment that was given to me. All of my classes were intriguing but it was in my African American Studies class that I thrived the most and found that I had a voice of inspiration to others. As I was still in the process of learning myself and growing my confidence, I encouraged my classmates, which essentially empowered me. I was also taking a Study of Religions course, that pushed me in a direction of strengthening my spirituality. For some time, I had lost hope in the belief that there was someone protecting me and looking out for me, but I took some time to reevaluate my feelings based on the things I was learning. I realized just how important it was to me to pray and believe in something bigger than myself. I started to take my relationship with God more seriously. I truly desired to understand what it really meant to love God and how to talk to him. There was finally a difference in how I prayed, because I started to believe in what I prayed for. I really believed in the things I asked God for and I was starting to see evidence of his answers every day. I was praying for forgiveness and letting go of the anger I had inside. Even though I was having the time of my life being on my own, I often thought about Dad and Shirl and Kim. I would have dreams about meeting Gwen and Dad being in love with her. Those dreams then turned into nightmares of Gwen standing with Shirl while she beat me. Gwen would then reappear with Kim and smile as she yelled at me and called me stupid. These dreams would play like a movie reel each night and I would wake up in a sweat, trying to shake the images. I think my roommate was convinced that I was crazy because I was always so shaken after waking up and she swore I was hallucinating. I thought about the story someone told me when I was younger about how Gwen broke Dad's heart and he was never the same after they split. I didn't think that I still had a desire to be a family with Dad but I often felt pity for him and the possibility of him acting out because of a broken heart. I now understood what it felt like to be hurt by someone you loved romantically and I understood how love can sometimes make you become someone you never thought you would be. I constantly heard stories from my friends at school about how they were deceived but bounced back and refused to become bitter and angry. That was magical to me. Being able to live through the pain and become an even better person because of it is admirable. I strived for that rebirth daily and nightly, fighting the images and reminders of the people that hurt me. I clung to my writing for peace and prayed constantly for the confidence to do what I was most afraid to do. I knew that I truly desired a relationship with Gwen, and I couldn't keep denying it, so I decided to contact her. I got her phone number from Charity and told her that I would call when I finished all my classes for the day. Charity thought it was a great idea for me to call because she would always tell me that Gwen asked about me constantly. I wondered why she asked about me but never tried to get in touch with me. I shook that thought away and pushed myself to focus on being positive when I spoke with her. I finished my last class and headed straight to my room. I had a bag of chips in my hand and some gummy worms to snack on later. I grabbed my small blanket off the foot of my bed and plopped down on the couch in the living room space. My roommate had to work after her class, so I knew I had the place to myself for a bit. I quickly dialed Gwen's number and my heart started to beat faster. My stomach felt queasy and I had forgotten everything that I practiced. The phone continued to ring as I scrambled for my notebook where I jotted a few things down; then the line clicked and I heard a hoarse voice say "Hello."

 "Hello." I echoed back. "Can I speak to Gwen?" I asked.

"This is her", the hoarse voice replied.

I was nervous and didn't know what to say next. All I heard was breathing as I waited for her to say something. She started to cough into the phone and slightly wheeze. "Are you ok?" I awkwardly asked. She didn't reply. I waited for her to speak but there was just silence. " This is Vivian, and

I was calling to speak to you and see how you were doing," I said shyly. Gwen replied by saying, she knew it was me and that she was happy to hear my voice. "How is school going?" she added. "I love school, I'm having a great time and learning a lot!" I said with a smile. "I'm so happy to hear that," Gwen said softly. The conversation lightened as I told her about my classes and the things I was learning. She silently listened. I looked down at my paper to see if there was another question I could ask. "Can you tell me what happened with you and Dad?" I asked nervously, squeezing my eyes shut. There was a small pause before she answered. "I would love to tell you that everything was great with us, but it wasn't. I don't want you to hate your father for me not being around. I fought to be there for you guys, I really did. I did have a hard time because I was on drugs and I'm not proud of it. I listened intently as she spoke. "There were times that I wanted to just hold you,

you were just a baby. But because I wasn't my usual self, your Dad wouldn't let me. He was protecting you guys and I don't blame him. That's all you should know." She said calmly.

I was in tears on the other side of the phone. I was completely silent as I digested her words.

She continued to detail her current struggles with being addicted to crack but wanting to stop.

"I was in rehab for a while and my sponsor was helping me to stay clean but I kept running back into the dealer. Next thing I know, I'm strung out again. Happens all the time like a cycle." She mumbled. I could tell it hurt her to say this to me.

 Anger rose in my body as I wiped tears from my face. "Who sells it to you?" I said sternly. "I want to know a name!"

There was silence.

"Mom?" I said loudly, it slid off my lips.

"What is their name?" I demanded as if I could do something to change things.

I could hear her breathing heavily, then she said my name softly:

"Vivian, ...the dealer's name is Stone."

16: "Can I call you?"

I grabbed the remote on the edge of the table and turned the tv on. I had to do something, anything to calm me down. I was in disbelief that my family was the reason why my mother was strung out on drugs. My own family that talked about how bad of a mother she was for not being around. That family. I had been living in a fantasy world, believing that everyone loved the sane way I did, but just showed it differently. I was wrong. I thought that being away at school healed me and that people were no longer going to hurt me because I was stronger. I was wrong about that too. I took a real blow that day.

The phone call with Gwen brought a lot of anger and resentment back to the surface. A few weeks after my heartfelt conversation with her, I got into a disagreement with Aunt Viv. I was made aware that I needed to call Dad and that it was important to keep up with him. I was mortified at her expecting me to do that after everything I had been through with him. I was trying to explain to her that I wasn't interested in contacting certain people for a while. She knew how disappointed I was after being accepted to college and not hearing anything from him. He hadn't helped me get into school or even thought to send me a couple dollars to get things I needed. But I was supposed to contact him and see how he's doing? I couldn't understand why the responsibility always fell on me to keep in touch with people. I thought to myself one day, after attending my classes: "Why am I so hurt when my aunt doesn't understand me or take up for me?" I wanted her to see that I was trying my best to forgive. I wished that someone would just give me a break and let me feel how I wanted to feel. This was too much to ask for from from my family. My aunt was frustrated with my decisions and attitude after our conversation, so she refused to reach back out to me for weeks. I realized why I was so hurt by her not understanding me and even cutting me off for weeks. I placed my aunt in a role that was never hers and expected her to perform actions that didn't come naturally. After some time of living with my aunt, I naturally began to call her Mom. It wasn't something that someone told me to do, it was a feeling that I got when I was around her. She was there for me in times when no one else was. But it was after going off to school that I realized the difference in my connection and the ones that my friends had with their moms. There was such a desperation factor involved in me calling my aunt, mom. I wanted to be loved on that level of a daughter but just didn't know how to get it. She was the closest thing I had to a mom. There were times that I felt misunderstood and confused about my relationships but having her around, helped me cope. During college, I had been searching for a true connection to the people in my life and my family. But when I closed my eyes and thought of the definition of love, Gwen's face was the one that appeared. Along with the faces of my brother, sister and grandfather. They were the only ones that still represented happiness to me.

I was evolving into the woman I always dreamed of becoming. College changed me forever. I spent sacred days creating lasting friendships, pledging a sorority that reassured me of my purpose, and nurturing the kind of confidence that prepared me to love again. I consumed myself with being excellent in school and refused to allow issues from my family to distract me, which was easier said than done.

I was proud of my accomplishments, my grades were top of the line and I was finally confident in who I was and it showed. There were guys on campus who were interested in me but no one had all of my attention. One night, my line sisters and I partied at our favorite spot in Greensboro. Our game plan was solid: we go in together, and we leave together.

We walked in and headed straight for the bathroom, just to catch another glimpse of how fabulous we looked, then ventured to the bar to grab a cocktail. We scoped the place, bouncing in sync along to the jams we all loved, then finally headed to the dance floor to get the party started. We traveled in a pack, like wolves on a mission, so we were totally inseparable. Whenever we went to the club and someone would stop one of us to chat, they would end up getting cut short. We never gave out our numbers and usually left our phones in the car to eliminate the need to explain ourselves. Our sole purpose was to dance the night away in a cute little circle, forgetting about all the stress from group projects and class assignments that plagued us through the week. We were always asked to dance but like clockwork, after the one song ended, it was back to the cute little circle we danced in. This particular night, nothing went as it usually did. A couple of us were asked to dance and ventured off, but no one rejoined the circle after they finished dancing.

I felt a hand embrace mine and pull me gently to the middle of the dance floor. I felt the beat permeating through my body and I leaned in, lending my curves to him as we danced slowly and he held me close. He whispered in my ear, asking what school I went to and I mouthed "WSSU." He gazed at me, then laughed and said he was appalled by my choice of college, but nevertheless, intrigued by me. I knew, without asking, where he went to school. Our schools were rivals. I giggled playfully and we exchanged a few details about ourselves as we continued to dance. The

DJ scratched the record and got on the mic, "This is the last song of the night, make it good people! Fellas! Find you a cutie and get that dance!"

The mystery guy reached for my hand once again and I decided there was no harm in breaking the "no consecutive dance rule", that my girls and I established earlier that year. I shrugged my shoulders and allowed him to guide me back to the center of the club. We had a full conversation with our bodies under the flashing neon lights. We let the bass tremble under our feet and guide our moves. Before the song ended, he leaned in and asked for my number. I glanced around me and there was no one to interfere so I left my number with him, then scurried away like Cinderella leaving the ball.

A few days later, a text came through that read: "Hey this is Maurio, how are you?" I shook my head and smirked. "That's the guy from the club", I thought to myself. My phone vibrated once again and I looked down to see: "Can I call you?"

I stopped what I was doing and plopped down on my bed, holding my phone in my hand. It wasn't often that guys wanted to talk on the phone. It was usually through text, so I sat there shocked, but all the while, amused. I quickly texted back, "Yes, you can", then a few minutes later, my phone rang. I hesitated, trying to think of something witty to say but I couldn't. I made sure to remember his name: Maurio. I remembered it well because my favorite game when I was younger was Mario Kart. I giggled at my reference to his name. When I heard his voice, I was nervous about what to say and he proceeded to ask me about my day. Again, I was completely taken aback, by his questions, but I showed no sign of it. That night we stayed on the phone for two hours like teenagers with new phones. We talked about everything! From family to love to sex and religion, the conversation was impressive and it blew my mind. I felt twice as guilty for not expecting much from the conversation since we met at the club.

 I was turned on by his ambition. He wasn't like any guy that I had met before and I could sense a soft side to him but of course, it was covered up by this rough appeal that he portrayed. Two hour conversations became a regular thing for us. Weeks flew by and we both craved the amazing conversations we had daily. We slowly became more open with each other and anticipated spending more time together.

We started out as friends and took our relationship slow, agreeing that jumping into anything wasn't the best idea for either one of us. Maurio had recently gotten out of an unhealthy relationship. He mentioned briefly how in his previous relationship, they would continually argue but he hated arguing.

"How do you argue if you hate it?" I asked. "What did you argue about?" I persisted. I was curious to know every detail. He would usually divert the conversation, insisting on only talking about things that made me happy and contributed to what we were building. I loved that but I still wanted to know. I craved to know all the things that made him who he was. I wanted the entire story, no matter how ugly it was. After getting to know Maurio, I could tell that he was broken, as I was. Fortunately, I became an expert at disguising my brokenness so I could point it out easily in others. In the beginning of our relationship, I would always say things like, "You look so good." He would always reply: "No I don't, or yeah right, you lying." It was weird at first hearing a guy say that but deep down I knew what the issue was. He was a reflection of me and everything I was working on leaving behind. He reminded me of my Dad, and all the reasons I still loved him, despite the past. "So, what if he is broken", I told myself. We could grow and build together, and create a life where we never have to go back to the people that broke us down. That sounded ideal to me.

Maurio and I would stay up late at night, looking up at the ceiling, telling each other all our dreams and all the crazy ideas we kept locked away. It was some of the most freeing moments in my life, where I didn't have to think twice about being myself. We became lovers and healers for each other. Neither of us could have imagined how attached we would become but our connection was so incredibly beautiful. I believed in Maurio more than he believed in himself and he believed in me more than I believed in myself. It was an interesting connection that we had, although, as we became even more serious, Maurio doubted

the man he could be for me. We toyed with the idea of

seeing other people but neither one of us could stay away

from each other. He didn't realize that meeting him

changed everything for me.

17: "Do you still love me?"

"I'm not able to finish school." I cried. Maurio rubbed my back slowly as I sobbed loudly. They told me that I reached my maximum funding with my financial aid, can you believe that?" I yelled. "I should have never changed my major! I should have just graduated and went back to school for something I love more." I added. I was overwhelmed at all that was coming at me at once. My car had recently broke down and I didn't have the money to get it fixed. I was now without transportation and unable to complete my degree. I was devastated. "Everything is going to work out for you babe, it always does." Maurio encouraged. He just completed his very last semester of school and was preparing for graduation. I felt awful for bringing all my problems to him when he was supposed to be celebrating but I had no one else to talk to. "I'm sorry for all this babe, I am just so hurt right now." I explained.

"Don't apologize, you are perfectly fine. I hope you know I'm walking across that stage for the both of us. You know it hasn't been easy for me either." He reminded me. "The struggle is real, but Goddd is Able!" He proclaimed in his best preacher voice. I couldn't help but laugh. He was always good at helping me redirect my energy to a more positive space. We were going on 3 years of dating and he constantly found new ways to make me smile. Throughout our college experience, we had a chance to take trips together, we met each other's' family and we continued to push each other in our personal goals. Graduation was a goal that we both shared and worked so hard for. The day that he walked across the stage and earned his degree was the day I realized just how much I was invested in our relationship. It felt like I had graduated as well.

Despite everything I had going on, Maurio gave me hope that things would get better. Shortly after graduation, he moved back home to Charlotte to pursue an opportunity in his career field. It was a big time for him because he had worked so hard to gain employment with one of the biggest companies in construction. I stayed in Winston for a couple of months, doing my best to salvage the vehicle I had and find loopholes in order to complete my degree. I eventually made the hard decision to move back home to Charlotte and leave the place that brought so much freedom and love to my life. The only exciting part of my return was to be in Maurio's arms more consistently. I was missing him tremendously while in Winston, so it made the decision a lot easier to move back. I slowly sunk into a depression shortly after my return home. I moved back in with my grandparents. The transition was difficult for me because I was no longer living in my own place and no longer had my own form of transportation. I was dependent on my family once again and was reminded of it every day.

Grandma would complain about everything that I did. She complained about how long I took a shower or how I didn't have any money to be getting a second helping of food. I didn't understand how she was always so stuck on the cost of everything. On top of being ridiculed by my family, I received a phone call about Gwen being gravely sick and that she didn't have much time left. This was a hard punch in my stomach. I kept contact with Gwen while in school and did my best to go see her whenever I came home, but because I didn't come home often, it had been awhile since I seen her face.

I couldn't believe the news, and immediately felt ashamed for not being in touch. The last conversation we had was one I wish I could forget. She was high when she called my number, and she asked me if I had any money to give her. I honestly didn't have any to spare but would have been willing to, if I did. She repeatedly told me that I only call her when I want things so I should be helping her. It was disheartening to have to hang up on her but I couldn't let anything take me back to that scary, and hateful place I used to reside. Despite our few pleasant encounters, she was still the woman that gave birth to me and there was a big part of me that needed her at that moment in my life. Gwen struggled with her drug addiction throughout my time in college so it was difficult to develop a true relationship with her while she manipulated my emotions in order to get money for drugs. I continued to love her the best way I could but it never fulfilled me the way I desired.

I talked with Brian and Charity and they filled me in on what I missed in my absence. She became sick over the last year and it escalated quickly, causing her body to become too weak to walk or even sit. I was doing my best to process everything as it came at me abruptly upon my return. Brian suggested that I go by her mom's house to see her, while he was there. I arrived and immediately noticed how small she had gotten but she smiled as I entered the room and I could tell she was happy to see me. I sat on the edge of the bed and reached for her hand. As soon as her hand touched mine, the tears began to pour. "Don't you do that." She scolded me as she laid there. I closed my eyes and exhaled loudly. There was something about holding her hand that took me back to middle school when I felt so alone and when I felt like I had no one.

I wiped my eyes, then glanced up at all the doodles and frames she made that now hung on the walls. I listened to her as my eyes gazed at the intricate details of her drawings, then back to her again. Her voice lightened as she talked about how happy she was to see me so in love with Maurio. "You remind me of myself, loving your Dad."

She said softly. She continued : "All of my kids were born, relentless lovers with an undying love in their hearts."

I knew that I loved just as deep as she did.

She reminded me of who I was. A lover.

She knew that I was battling with so much at that moment but refused to pry. There was silence.

I saw myself within those four walls and it frightened me. As joyous as I was to finally be sharing time together, I couldn't fight the thought of my life possibly reflecting hers. It was a terrible thought to have, to even ponder at that moment, but I questioned if my heart would leave me lonely as hers had. And would I be left only to reminisce and daydream of the good times instead of living them until my last moment?

"Do You Still Love Me?" Gwen startled me out of my thoughts.

I hesitated before answering, swallowing the words said to me.

"Of course, I do. I stuttered. I have never stopped loving you."

"You know, I've never stopped loving your Dad?" She revealed. Her mouth curled into a slight grin as she shifted her body against the stiff pillows that lay along her back. "He could come back today and if he asked me to try again, I would say yes."

I smiled at her, marveling at the thought of looking past all the pain and hurt someone caused and inviting them back into your life. It seemed almost impossible to me. "I always wondered why you would still love me, knowing that I wasn't who you needed me to be," she said as she looked downward, shaking her head.

"I wasn't there for you guys and your Dad, he never gave me a chance to be there. I always wanted you to know how much I loved you but I was scared because I was afraid of what you thought of me." She bit her lip. "I was afraid that you were embarrassed of me because I was on drugs."

Silence permeated the room for a moment.

"Well, are you, embarrassed of me?" She stammered.

I sighed, doing my best to steady my breathing. I was still prone to anxiety attacks whenever I felt uncomfortable and forced to say things I didn't feel.

"I understand what you've been through, so no, I'm not." I lied.

Tears trickled down my face without warning, my heart pounded against my ribcage and I closed my eyes in an attempt to manage my anxiety but I couldn't seem to hold in my pain any longer.

"Life has been hell without you! I stammered.

I can't sit here and say I'm fine because I'm not!" I bawled my fists in protest. I'm angry! I'm hurt! I shouted, marching over to the window. And Yes, I'm embarrassed! I've gone my entire life feeling like neither of my parents wanted me! Do you know how that feels?" I turned around, my face scrunched in anger.

"Have you ever felt like no one would care if you left this world?" My voice cracked. Do you know how heavy that burden is?"

"And have you ever doubted God? Have you ever questioned why he allowed things to happen to you?" I peered into her bloodshot, red eyes.

"Wait, don't answer that." I turned away, rubbing my trembling hands together.

"Well, I have." I whimpered, then turned back to face her.

"If there was nothing else, I believed in us. I believed in your love as my Mother, no matter what I was told growing up! Despite how many horror stories I have lived through, I never gave up hope that you loved me like no one else

could." I said, blinking back tears.

"I never stopped loving you Mom." I weeped.

18: "She waited for you."

As the organ played, numerous people paced down the church aisle towards the casket, paying their last respects to my Mom. The air was filled with screams and wails. Sadness moved swiftly, latching onto everyone who entered. My eyes settled on all the people that talked bad about her but were never willing to help. There were so many people from her neighborhood there, that appeared to be distraught. The front row is where I sat alongside Brian and Charity, numb and silent. The pastor made the announcement that they would be closing the casket and to please come up now if you choose to view the body. The church erupted in shouts, with everyone whimpering loudly as they came down the aisle. "Why Lord Jesus? Why? Not her Lord, not her!"

I sat there motionless, gave an eye to Charity, then looked ahead once more at people putting on a show. At that moment, I embodied every hurt and pain that Gwen had taken from others. I imagined how she felt as she watched this display take place. Where was this love when she was living? My heart broke into pieces. I watched as others continued to hang their heads and whimper. They jumped up and down as if the Holy Spirit had gotten into them and hollered as the casket permanently closed. The ushers motioned for everyone to return to their seats. I rolled my eyes as I wiped them with kleenex; dreading the fact that we had to sit through another display of this at the cemetery after we left this precession. I had run out of tears and I couldn't wait for this day to end.

After Gwen passed, I felt completely lost. I had to face the stinging reality of my mother dying, and never getting a chance to have a real relationship with her. My thoughts were all over the place and there were days that I couldn't bring myself to even get out of bed. Maurio would hold me for as long as he could. Weeks passed and all I felt was numbness. I thought about what the future looked like for my siblings. I thought about what if it was one of us, would anyone care what we had been through? The one person we hoped would care, didn't even show up to our Mom's funeral. Dad never even called us to see if we were alright. My thoughts would constantly replay the moment I entered the hospital room and was told that she just took her last breath. "She waited for you." Charity told me. I just stood there comforting her and Brian in that hospital room. My arms held them but my mind wasn't even there anymore. This was the end of this story, I thought. There was no use exhausting any more energy questioning and piecing things together to make sense for my life. I tried to pick up the pieces, settling with the thought that I still had my father but I felt lost with him too. I had been holding onto a promise of "everything will get better", my entire life but it was such a false reality that I built hope on. My hope lingered deep in the unwavering love I had for Dad. I buried it years ago, but I knew exactly where to find it when I needed it. And I needed it at that moment. I needed him but he was nowhere to be found. His silence stuck the knife deeper into my chest as each day went by. I continued to mourn in bewilderment of how someone could continually hurt me deeply over and over again.

Then, as usual, I considered his feelings and what he might be experiencing. I did my best to analyze why Dad acted the way he did.

When Dad looks at me, he sees Gwen. His favorite lover, his best friend, his biggest failure. No one knew him like she did, and he never revealed himself to anyone like he did to her. As a child I caught a quick glimpse of the man he was but as I grew older, a surface version of him became all I knew. There had to be more to Dad than what I had seen and I refused to believe that love was not inside of him. In order to cope with the pain of his absence, I created my own understanding for his actions. I hardened like never before and refused to hide behind smiles or fake hugs any longer, it got to be too much. My anger and anxiety continued to escalate and I no longer wanted to be that sweet little Vivian that everyone knew me as.

I made a trip over to my grandparents house one evening. I forced myself to stop by after hearing multiple times that I was "acting different for not coming around." That visit made everything worse for me. I had been in such a low place, trying my best to deal with the emptiness I felt of Gwen being gone. I had yet to receive a phone call from anyone after months of mourning, so I felt as if no one really cared. The only communication I had was with Charity, Brian and Maurio.

"Hi Stranger." My Grandma belted out immediately after I entered the house.

"Where you been? She added.

"I've been around." I replied softly.

"I told your Dad, we ain't heard from ya." My grandma continued.

My body tensed up and I bit my lip, fighting back the curse words that swirled on my tongue.

I replied nonchalantly: "You heard from my Dad, oh that's real nice, because I haven't."

"Yeah he called, something you done forgot how to do." She snapped back.

I glared in her direction for a moment and noticed that my hands began to shake. As I continued to stare at her, my heart pounded rapidly and all I wanted to do was scream.

"My Mom recently passed away, just in case you forgot." I retorted loudly. No one has called to see how me, or Charity and Brian are doing at all." I said.

"Well I didn't know it was affecting you that much, seeing how she wasn't around." my aunt chimed in.

My grandma twisted herself in her chair. "She didn't do much for ya anyhow, if it wasn't for us, yall wouldnt of had nothing growing up."

Everyone stared at me as my breathing became heavier. My heart felt like it was going to throb out of my chest.

"What's wrong with you?" My aunt asked.

I couldn't pull myself to reply. My body continued to shake as I walked towards the door and reached for my keys to leave. I didn't even know how I got to the door so fast, I was just there and I walked out without saying goodbye.

I drove to the nearest gas station and broke down crying relentlessly. I looked out at the dark sky and slowly wiped my tears away.

 I was completely exhausted from trying to explain myself to everyone and please my family by being present without mindfully being present.

I was hurting and could no longer pretend that I was ok. Because I wasn't.

19: "What is your definition of Love?"

It wasn't until I admitted that I longed for a relationship with Gwen, did I really come to terms with how much pain was in my heart for her absence. I believe that I was in cold shock, after her death. I was looking around to see what other people were doing and trying to find a way to imitate it, because my emotions were unpredictable. Crying wasn't my initial response. I cried at her funeral but those tears were just the surface level of pain I felt. The deeper layers weren't revealed until months later. There was something caught in my throat and it was the pain that I had been holding onto for 28 years.

I made a decision to finally seek therapy.

I didn't know what to expect at my first therapy session, but it is one that I'll never forget. As I walked through the door, a sweet voice told me to make myself comfortable. I sat down in a gray sofa chair and leaned back, lifting my feet up from the ground. I couldn't help but notice all the festive decorations in her office. My therapist walked into the room slowly with two glasses of water in her hand. She handed me one of the glasses and smiled. As she sat down in her plush, grey chair, she introduced herself and told me that she had been a therapist for 15 years. I nodded and smiled nervously.

"What would you like to talk about?" She asked.

"There's just so much, I don't really know where to start." I stammered.

"Let's talk about what is happening right now in your life." She said calmly.

The first thing that stumbled out my mouth was the recent death of Gwen and how it brought me into her office.

"I don't know how to handle my emotions any more and I need help sorting them out." I declared.

I talked about my anger and how I was having more anxiety attacks. I was lost on how to deal with all of it, in addition to sorting out my feelings with family.

She was so in tune with everything I was saying, as she nodded and listened intently. Once all of my emotions began to pour out of me, we had come to the close of my first session. As I regained my composure, I realized just how comfortable and safe I felt at that moment. I left that day, feeling like a weight had been lifted from my shoulders. I needed that purge more than ever and I found peace in finally saying everything I felt, aloud.

As my therapy sessions continued, there were some days that I was left sick to my stomach after leaving. I would go straight home and ask Maurio to come over and stay with me. Some nights he would hold me as I cried. The wounds were fresh again and the last thing I wanted to be was alone. I needed his love more than ever. With each session, we continued to make connections to the things that happened in my childhood. I learned that there was no time limit on grief or how you're supposed to grieve.

Months flew by and I was feeling so much happier. I was coming into an understanding of myself and finally getting back to the things that I loved. I was writing again, and reading books that brought a smile to my face. Therapy gave me all the time I needed to heal. My therapist made sure to remind me of how worthy I was of everything I desired from life; that meant so much.

I arrived for my last session of therapy and I made a point to reflect on my progress and my feelings. My spirits were lifted and I was ready to move forward. My therapist looked at me and asked: "What is your definition of love?" I pondered this question after she said it to me and a smile slid across my face. For so long, I was used to spilling out definitions of different words but this particular one always gave me pause. This time I didn't have a definition but a story to share instead.

"I remember the day that I fell in love with Maurio. It was 2 years prior." I began with a grin. "We were riding in his beat-up car, down the street with the windows down because his AC didn't work. I was looking out the window and then back at him. He asked me how I was feeling since our conversation the night before. I'm not sure how we got on the topic of addictions but, the night before, I decided to share with him the history of my mother and my childhood as it was. I don't know what came over me but I wasn't shaking and I wasn't ashamed for the first time in my life. I didn't fear the bad reaction as I sat beside him, leaning up against the white wall in his room. He put his arm around me as I told him detail after detail and after I finished, he told me to stand up. I stood up and peered into his eyes.

"You are the most beautiful woman I know." He said gently, as he wiped the tears from my face. "And you is smart, you is kind, and you is important." He grinned as I revealed a smile. We stood there in the middle of his room and he held me forever."

"That is my definition of my love," I told my therapist.

"Coming to therapy with you has changed my life and I'm also glad that I had Maurio to push me through it." I said softly.

She instantly embraced me and we hugged for the last time. Her perfume lingered in the air as I left her office. It was the same perfume that Ms. Byrd wore.

Later that evening, I reflected on the story I told my therapist.

Falling in love is something that can happen unexpectedly, but the timing of Maurio coming into my life seemed to be spiritually coordinated. I was able to speak my truth to someone who could have easily judged me but instead, welcomed my freedom from the bondage of fear. All I wanted to do after that day, was love him with everything I had. I marvelled at how he was able to share with me in the same capacity. Maurio recognized his own flaws, saying them out loud and gradually opening up about the issues he struggled with. I think I loved him because he was broken and I saw myself within him. We were natural givers so our connection was a cycle of overflow. I made a decision to stop holding back on the love I so naturally wanted to give. I wasn't afraid anymore to let in love because I knew I deserved it no matter what I had been through.

Time had passed and Maurio and I continued to elevate our level of freedom with each other and the other relationships in our lives. We just finished having our traditional New Year's Eve dinner together, where we discussed resolutions and the diets we would start and stop a month later. We laughed and reminisced about all the great times we shared during the year. Afterwards, we decided to venture to a nearby park and celebrate by watching the fireworks mark the dawn of a new year. There were people dancing in the cold, excited and filled up with joy all around us. We cracked jokes at the tone deaf cover band that was butchering all of Michael Jackson's best hits. We sang along, in between laughs. I buried my face into Maurio's chest to get warm; it was extremely cold. He grabbed my hand and started to lead me to another area.

"Let's go sit down for a minute." He said, without waiting for an answer.

"Babe, I'm so cold and it's almost Midnight! We gotta get a good view." I protested.

"I know, we'll get back up before they start." He reassured me.

I followed him as he led me to a table with two chairs beside it. Christmas lights illuminated the area beautifully and a mistletoe hung conveniently right above us.

I sat down and instantly felt chills through my legs that quickly spread through my body. He laughed at my scrunched up face. I giggled back. I loved seeing him smile and looking at his face took my mind off the cold. He stared back at me for a few moments and then said:

"I love you Vivian."

"I love you too baby!" I chimed back enthusiastically. I gave him a strange look and asked him if he was ok. He nodded and slowly stood from his chair, and then lowered himself on one knee right in front of me. He looked at me just as he did the day I told him my story in his room, and he said strongly: "Vivian Elizabeth Jones, will you spend the rest of your life with me?"

I couldn't speak. My mouth opened but nothing came out at first.

"Oh my God." I whispered. I shook my head in disbelief. At that very moment, I thought about every single thing that had taken place in my life. I thought about all the things I could have allowed to break me but I persisted. I realized that it was all necessary. We both looked at each other with tears in our eyes, and I said Yes.

I said Yes to creating our own definition of love.

I said Yes to creating our very own story of survival and I said Yes to forgiving anyone who had ever hurt me. I knew at that moment, that there was no way I could hold on to such pain and still have enough room for the happiness I was destined to have.

I stood up after he placed the ring on my finger and I clung

to him, with so much joy in my heart.

"7-6-5-4-3-2…Happy New Year!"

People shouted all around us in triumph and joy. I looked at

the fireworks lighting up the sky.

 I smiled, closed my eyes and I said:

"I Forgive You."